SURVIVO

True stories of airmen who crashed – and lived to tell the tale

David Rowland

Best Wishes
David Rowland

𝓕𝓟

Finsbury Publishing

By the same author:
The Brighton Blitz
The Coastal Blitz
Out of the Blue
Spitfires Over Sussex: the Exploits of 602 Squadron
War in the City, part 1

Front cover: Painting of Halifax in sea off Seaford (Dugald Cameron).
Back cover: Heinkel He111 after a crash-landing near Worthing, Sussex.
Title page: A Nichols & Son lorry removing the remains of a Me109 to
. . . . Faygate, near Horsham in Sussex.

British Library Cataloguing-in Publication Data.
A catalogue record for this book is available from the British Library.

ISBN 0-9539392-3-5

Published by Finsbury Publishing, 2 Harvest Close, Telscombe Cliffs,
Peacehaven, East Sussex BN10 7JG

Printed by Pageturn Limited, Hove, BN3 7DX. 01273 821500

CONTENTS

Acknowledgements

Many people have supplied information, both written and verbal, for this book, while others have generously supplied pictures and photographs. My thanks to them all, with apologies to any I have inadvertently overlooked.

My very good friend from Scotland, Dugald Cameron, former principal of Glasgow College of Art, painted the cover picture for me from a few notes that I supplied and the co-operation of Halifax pilot Sam Liggett.

Trevor Evans, a retired Brighton fireman now living in Hurstpierpoint, set me on the trail of the Patcham B17 Flying Fortress, Winsome Winn II.

John Dibley, a former assistant chief constable cum historian, gave me invaluable information regarding the two Barcombe Junkers 88 aircraft crashes. He was also of great assistance with the Lewes Halifax crash.

Bob Elliston featured the story of that crash in his wonderful *Lewes at War 1939-1945*, one of the best books published about local wartime issues, and he kindly gave me additional information about it.

Adam Trimingham, of *Argus* fame, came to my aid by suggesting the title of the book when I was completely stumped – just as he had done for my last book, *Out of the Blue*.

David Arscott, a former senior producer for BBC Radio Brighton/Sussex, continues to edit my books with total professionalism. I applaud his patience with me as I wander through the realms of publishing.

Sally Blann and her team at the Brighton History Centre have given me continued help and assistance, and have also allowed me to publish a number of photographs in my books.

Since I first became involved in publishing I have been very lucky with a number of people offering me help and advice. I class all the above not only as experts in their particular fields, but as very dear and personal friends.

As for my wife Christine, she has once again allowed me to take over our lounge, reducing it to a total mess reminiscent of a tip, with copious pieces of paper, photographs and reference books scattered around.

David Rowland
Telscombe Cliffs

INTRODUCTION

"The RAF is the cavalry of modern war."
Stansky, Churchill.

I vaguely remember as a boy growing up in Brighton in the Second World War and hearing about an American bomber that had crashed at Patcham with, we were told, the loss of all the crew. I can recall wondering what those poor airmen must have thought just prior to being killed.

Wild and hugely graphic stories and rumours were often passed around during the war, and as children we would cheer when we heard that a German aircraft had crashed, especially if we heard that the crew had been killed. Some 60 years on it is perhaps difficult to imagine such feelings, but it was, after all, the Germans who were dropping bombs and trying to kill us.

The Patcham crash was a seed that grew in my mind and that led to my researching and writing about many more wartime incidents. I used to wonder how, why and where these aircraft had crashed. My original idea was to include only stories of aircraft that had come down in my native Sussex, although I soon realised that there were many more exciting stories to tell from further afield.

My researches began with that American bomber crash at Patcham, questioning what had happened to it, who the pilot was and how many of the crew had been killed. I managed to find a small report in the *Evening Argus,* which had been written around the time of the crash but which, because of wartime secrecy, contained little detail. I then had a marvellous piece of luck. I met up with Trevor Evans, a retired Brighton fireman who had himself spent a lot of time researching this American B17 bomber crash and had actually visited the scene.

The American bomber was a B17 Flying Fortress named Winsome Winn II, and it so happened that none of the crew had been killed after all. This was certainly due to the flying skills of the pilot, 2nd Lt. Norman DeFrees. Trevor Evans put me in touch with Luther Smith, who was the ball turret gunner, and lives in the USA.

1

Through him I made contact with Norman DeFrees, who, in September 1999 stayed with me at my home in Telscombe Cliffs. These two former members of the crew told me their stories of the fateful mission which ended with a crash-landing in a field above Braypool, Patcham, in the northern part of Brighton on Tuesday 8th February 1944.

They not only told their stories in a detailed and most graphic way but also gave an account of their next mission, when their aircraft was shot down over Germany: most of the crew were severely wounded (Luther Smith lost his hand) and became POWs.

Another American B17 Flying Fortress with severe engine trouble and a shortage of fuel just about managed to cross the Channel after a mission to Germany; before crashing at Beddingham, near Lewes. The crew managed to bale out over Southease. This story was told to me by Temp/Sgt Theodore (Dusty) Rhodes who was the top gunner on this aircraft, and who also lives in the USA.

Quite by accident I learned of another story, this being one of the most dramatic crash-landings of the war in this area. The pilot, Flt. Sgt. Sam Liggett, successfully ditched his huge and badly damaged Halifax bomber in the sea off Seaford, thus saving his crew. He has given me the full story, from the take-off from Breighton in Yorkshire to the final ditching in the sea. It includes the official story of the Halifax shooting down a German attacker while *en route* for home. He also tells of how the crew came together prior to their missions. In October 2000 I had the pleasure of meeting Sam at his home in Scotland, and we have become very firm friends.

The book features these and many other stories, including some from German pilots who were shot down over Sussex to become prisoners of war.

While I was researching material for the book *Spitfires over Sussex* I was fortunate to come into contact with members of 602 Squadron and with a number of other pilots who were involved in dog-fights over Sussex but were later shot down over enemy territory. These stories, I feel, are too good to leave out and I take personal pride in publishing them. Many of the pilots are not as well known to the general public as the likes of Douglas Bader or Johnnie Johnson, but that in no way detracts from the marvellous stories they relate. As in all walks of life, certain individuals stand out – and probably none more than Wg.-Cdr. Patrick 'Paddy' Barthropp. He was a mere 20 years old when he acted as the 'weaver' for 602 Squadron above Sussex, the most dangerous of jobs in formation flying.

He treated life in the most honest of ways, none more than when making out reports on his junior officers. One read: 'Flying Officer Harvey is a scruffy genius. He thinks he's a genius; I think he's scruffy.' Another reported that 'this officer spends most of his time pushing doors marked pull'. Paddy ended the war in Stalag Luft III, the POW camp made famous by the film 'The Great Escape'. He was a nuisance to the German guards right from the start and, as in the film, was sentenced to 28 days in the cooler.

There are stories, too, from Ken 'Mac' Mackenzie and Wallace Cunningham, who were shot down and joined Paddy in Stalag Luft III; from Bob Doe, a top fighter pilot who suffered a serious injury when he crash-landed; and from George 'Ben' Bennions and Geoffrey Page, two of Sir Archibald McIndoe's early 'guinea pigs,' who had

Heinkel He111 crash-landed at High Salvington, near Worthing in Sussex, on 16 August 1940 after being shot down by Joe Kayll. Two of the crew died and three were captured. [Kayll]

plastic surgery at East Grinstead after suffering serious injuries and horrendous burns. The brave Czech, Josef Frantisek, tells how he crash-landed in a field of cabbages and went on to become the top-scoring fighter pilot during the Battle of Britain.

We hear from Allan Wright, another top fighter pilot who has a story to tell, and from Joe Kayll, who was almost shot while still in the cockpit of his stationary Hurricane after having been brought down over France. He had his photo taken by an unknown person, who sent it to the RAF in England, informing the authorities of his capture.

I cannot leave out in this introduction the brave Polish pilot, Stanislaw Jozefiak, an air gunner whose aircraft crashed in Sussex, with the loss of three lives. Stanislaw returned to Sussex in his 80s and built a monument to his fallen colleagues on the spot where the aircraft crashed. He went on to learn how to fly fighters and by the end of the war was a Spitfire pilot: that's determination.

The object of the book is twofold – to recount a number of vivid first-hand stories and, in doing so, to introduce readers to little-known airmen who nevertheless had an exciting and incident-packed war. I am still in regular contact with many of them, although time marches on and each year more of them pass on to pastures new. Indeed, this year alone I have lost two more good friends in David Cox and George 'Ben' Bennions.

These brave men took up the cudgels on our behalf, to fight the foe and to bring freedom to all those persecuted in the world of the 1940s, particularly those who suffered under German occupation. I feel proud and privileged to be able to tell their stories in this book, and to be associated, in however small a way, with their lives.

Air Crash at Rottingdean

People walking on the downs near Rottingdean, Sussex, in July 1939 were alerted to a Hawker Hind two seater fighter plane flying quite low. It was obvious that the pilot had some sort of engine trouble. Several of the walkers stood and watched from a distance as the aircraft struck the side of the hill and then ran along the uneven downland for about 60 yards. The propeller struck the ground, causing the aircraft to overturn and sustain extensive damage.

The aircraft came down on Honeysuckle Hill, New Barn Farm, which was owned by Percy Filkins of Ovingdean Grange. The onlookers were too far away to be of any assistance to the pilot, Alan Geoffrey Page. Struggling from the aircraft, he made his way down towards Rottingdean and was taken to a local school, where he was treated by Dr. Frederick Webb for a severe laceration to his right hand. He was in considerable pain, and his flying kit was badly blood-stained.

The local police guarded the plane until relieved by RAF personnel: a local newspaper reported that 'police officers in a Flying Squad car' arrived at the scene and took charge.

The Hawker Hind on its back. Note the local policeman in his white helmet, guarding the aircraft. [Brighton Local Studies Library]

A witness later said: 'I thought the pilot would land in Happy Valley a short distance from the crash site, but he apparently decided that the ground there was too rough.'

Geoffrey Page himself said later in an interview: 'I found the engine spluttering as I dived at about 300mph. I turned over from using the main fuel tank to the reserve tanks but to no avail. When the nose of the plane struck the ground the machine went over and the joystick went through my right hand. I shut off the ignition and then managed to wriggle my way out on my back between the cockpit and the grass. If I had not shut off the ignition I should have had a very hot end.'

Alan Page at the scene of the Rottingdean crash, with his hand bandaged. [Brighton Local Studies Library]

FLYER BIOG

Alan Geoffrey Page was born in Boxmoor, Hertfordshire on 16th May 1920 and studied engineering at London University. At the time of the Rottingdean crash he was a student belonging to the University of London Air Squadron and attached to the RAF at Thorney Island. He was called up for military service in September 1939 and joined the air squadron at Northolt.

He was shot down on 18th August while attacking a formation of Dornier Do 17s over the Channel and baled out of his Hurricane into the sea, being very badly burned. He spent more than two years in hospital at East Grinstead, being one of Dr. McIndoe's famous 'guinea pigs'.

Late in 1942 he volunteered for service in North Africa but had to return to England as the heat had an adverse effect on his skin grafts. He joined the AFDU at Wittering. On 29th June 1943 he and Sqn Ldr James MacLachlan shot down six enemy aircraft in 10 minutes just south of Paris. On 30th July he was awarded the DFC.

He joined 122 Squadron in 1943, took command of 132 Squadron the following year and became Wing leader of 125 Wing in July 1944. At the end of September he crashed his aircraft and was hospitalised once again with back injuries.

On 22nd August that year he received a Bar to his DFC for ten victories, and on 29th December the DSO after he had added three more victories. On 23rd January 1948 the Order of Orange Nassau with Swords was conferred upon him by HM Queen of the Netherlands.

Fire in the Cockpit

Wartime pilots flirted with death after every take-off. No one knew what was in store for them in the skies as they went to meet the enemy. There was however, one principal fear in their minds, that of being trapped in a blazing cockpit and roasted alive before they were able to bale out – a fate which befell far too many pilots during their combats. The pain and the fear they experienced we can merely guess at.

There were many third-degree burns victims among the pilots. To the good fortune of many, there was a remarkable doctor on hand who, during the summer of 1940, pioneered major improvements in the treatment of serious burns and in plastic surgery for the burns sufferers. Archibald McIndoe, later to be knighted by King George VI for his services to Britain, was a New Zealander who set up the trail-blazing burns unit in the Queen Victoria Hospital at East Grinstead, Sussex.

Cyril Jones, a leading aircraftsman, recalled: 'I was an operating assistant at the hospital. We were a 'Specialised Unit of Burns and Reconstructive Surgery.' We received members of the ground crew who were burnt as a result of German bombings and accidents on the airfields, as well as the pilots injured and burnt during combat.

'The pilots came mostly because of flash burns caused by high octane spirits from their fuel tanks. The burns were up to 60 or 70 per cent of their bodies. The difference between being burnt to a cinder and coming to the burns hospital might have been just three seconds exposure to the flames in a burning aircraft.

'Usually on Monday mornings McIndoe would fly around to all the main hospitals to decide which cases would be brought back to the hospital for treatment. After Dunkirk, we started treating burns victims with saline baths. We found that people with burns who had been immersed in salt water at Dunkirk did very well. Before that,there were some terrible things done. They had been using tannic acid and tannic jelly, which solidified over the burns. It was thought at this time that if you could cover the burn by excluding air, it wouldn't hurt so much. The tannic acid formed a film, but in addition to sealing out the pain, it sealed in the bacteria. All the germs and pus were locked inside the wound and there was a very high infection rate.

Another of the treatments involved 'gentian violet,' a violet dye that looked fluorescent when it was painted on. What it did was to make everything go rigid. There was a Canadian lad in the RAF whose leg had to be amputated above the knee because of the infection caused by the gentian. McIndoe stopped all that sort of treatment when he went over to the use of saline bath treatment, though there was still the danger that the burn victim might die of toxaemia or shock, the critical time being during the first 10 days after receiving his injuries.

Most of the patients were young men, young people in the prime of their lives. Most had been good looking before receiving their terrible injuries. The pilots who came to us were well educated, and to look the way they did after being so badly burned was very upsetting; it hit them very hard. You might have lost a leg, but in the

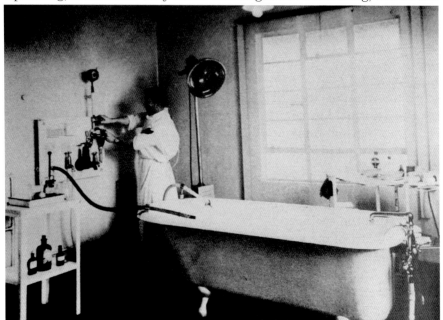

The saline bath introduced by McIndoe to ease the airmen's terrible burns.

next bed was a chap who'd lost his hands. A man might have no ears, but then there was another chap who was blind. It was all so terrible to see those young men in that condition.

'McIndoe insisted on putting these men together. He would never allow ranks to get special privileges. He was always being asked by other services to take special cases. We once had a captain in the Royal Navy who needed treatment. The Navy in those days were all posh. There was a lot of tradition and this, that and the other and, of course, the under ranks weren't even spoken of. The captain came to us one day: he'd lost an eye and McIndoe was asked to rebuild his eye socket. McIndoe admitted him into a ward with ordinary airmen who had suffered serious burns. The captain, who expected VIP treatment, was put into a ward with 40 men. On one side was a leading aircraftsman, on the other, a sergeant. Well, this Navy captain was in high dudgeon about it. He went to McIndoe and said, 'It is ridiculous for me to be nursed in a ward where I've got ordinary ranks around me. I must have a private room of my own.' McIndoe told him, ' You asked to be treated by me. If you wish to be treated by me, you will have the treatment I am offering. If you don't like the ward, then go and find someone else to treat you.'

'There was always terrific camaraderie among the patients; you would often see 15 wheelchairs being pushed into town, all going to the pub. McIndoe wanted the men to be accepted by the general public as normal human beings. He desperately wanted to give them back their normal functions and their dignity. In the early days, we had to go through the stage of men not wanting to live. Fully understandable. They were terrible to look at, but to see them now, after so many years – they are accepted, and have been for years.

'Some of them had to endure as many as 60 operations. Some decided that their wife accepts them and that was good enough. This is where many of the young girls married those men when they were at their worst.

'In his treatment McIndoe paid most attention to eyelids and hands. He would take a single layer of epidermis from the arm of the man to replace his eyelids. He wasn't looking to give a man back his looks, it just couldn't be done. He was however, aiming to restore their normal functions, such as opening and closing of the eyes, opening and closing of their mouths, restoring their noses and restoring the use of their hands. They went through phases. From healing the burns to starting reconstructive surgery could be anything from three days to three years.'

Dan Attwater, who was director of nursing at the Queen Victoria Hospital, said some of the men became customers for life. Scar tissue contracted after a while, and people therefore felt a tightening of the eyelids and a puckering of the mouth, so they had to keep having corrective surgery operations.

'It would be wrong of me to say we weren't horrified,' remarked Ann Standen, who was a nurse at the Queen Victoria. 'Inwardly, you would say, "Oh my God, what will they do with them?" You didn't recoil in horror, but you did wonder what could be done for them. Faces were just horrible, even the man I would later marry. He was injured when his bomber was in collision, the injuries were horrific. By the time he called a halt to the treatment and said enough was enough, he had new eyelids, a new nose and new lips. They couldn't do much for his hands because they were too badly burned. It was truly amazing what they did manage to do, incredible. At this stage he had undergone 60 operations.

'Relatives of the patients would come to the hospital to see the men. Some of them took it quite well but some didn't. It was too

---

FLYER BIOGS

Sqn. Ldr. Thomas Percy Gleave (RAF No. 29137) was 32 years old when he was shot down about 1pm on Saturday 31st August 1940 near Hazel Wood, Mace Farm, Cudham. He was admitted to Orpington Hospital badly burned and was later transferred to Queen Victoria Hospital. Four Hurricanes of 253 Squadron were shot down in this combat, with one pilot killed. He ended his RAF career as a group captain. A president of the Guinea Pig Club, he died in 1993.

Flying Officer Peter Frederick McDonald Davies (RAF No. 40088) was just 21 years old when he was shot down about 4.15pm on Tuesday 13th August 1940 by Me110s over Sheppey. Four Hurricanes of 56 Squadron were lost in this combat but no pilots were killed. Peter Davies ended his RAF career as a squadron leader and died in 1993.

---

much of a shock, just too much to take in and understand. They had seen a perfectly normal being one day and the next time they saw them, they were just a mess. They couldn't recognise them; it was such a terrible shock.

'Some of the men showed a tinge of bitterness, saying, "Why did it happen? – I'm finished now". They were soon made to realise that they were not the only ones with these terrible injuries."

Sqn. Ldr. Thomas Gleave.

Squadron Leader Tom Gleave, of 253 Squadron recounted what happened to him.

'There were long lines of Junkers Ju88s, possibly Heinkel's as well – huge grills of them stretching out in the sky. We had come too late to get above them, but we wanted to get them before they unloaded their bombs. We were climbing higher and higher; I could see everything on the aircraft above me, even the rivets. I broke my chaps away for the attack. I got onto no. 5 bomber on the outside line and fired, just beneath the nose. I couldn't get no. 4, but I gave no. 3 a burst. As I went over the top of him, I saw glycol pouring out of his engine. I went down to do number one bomber in line. I got a chink in my starboard tank – an incendiary – and it burst into flames.

'It burnt so quickly, it was unbelievable. I tried to get the cockpit hood open. Though I'd always been a stickler for drill, I forgot that all I had to do was to pull the toggle. I finally managed to get the hood open. By then I had undone my belt. As the hood came back, there was a God Almighty explosion. I went straight up in a huge sheet of flame. My aircraft had completely disappeared and I came down head over heels. I was able to pull my ripcord, and fortunately my parachute opened. I was pretty badly burned, about 30 per cent. All the skin of my right foot had gone; skin was missing from my face and one of my hands. My nose and eyelids were gone.

'We carried loaded guns and we could quite easily have shot ourselves. I would have done if I had ever reached the stage where I hadn't a hope in hell. I am sure some pilots did.

'One day, Sister came in [at the hospital] and told me that my wife had arrived. By this time I was well enough to worry about her seeing me as I was. My hands, forearms and legs were encased in dried tannic acid. My face, which felt the size of the proverbial melon, was treated in the same way, and I peered through slits in the mask.

'I heard footsteps approaching the bed and then saw my wife standing, gazing at me. She flushed a little and said, "What on earth have you been doing to yourself, darling?" I found it difficult to find the right words to answer her, but after a few seconds blurted out, "Had a row with a German".'

The hands of FO Peter Davies of 56 Squadron were badly burned and extremely painful when he had to bale out.

'They sprayed them with tannic acid and it formed a dark brown hard casing over my hands. The skin began to grow back over some of the fingers together and they had to be separated. One or two things went septic, but even so I recovered pretty quickly and I was fortunate compared to some of the other men – they were in a terrible state. There was another pilot officer named Davies who was brought in. His mother was very upset on seeing him. He was so badly burnt, his eyes were just slits. They brought her in to see me, to show her how burn cases could recover.'

Some 60 years after the Battle of Britain one cannot help but admire all those brave young men who went to war on the biggest stage of all – the skies. The figures in this battle are both staggering and awesome. We lost more than 1,000 aircraft but, more important, we lost in excess of 500 airmen. (The Luftwaffe lost more than 2,000 aircraft and more than 2,500 men.) I am pretty certain that people of today do not realise the full cost in lives during those few short months in 1940 – those rather famous months which ensured that we would be free.

A Lucky Day for Jack

This is a wonderful story told by a young 20 year old pilot who suddenly found himself having to act quickly in order to save his life. It was his first parachute jump under pressure. With enemy aircraft all around him, Pilot Sergeant Frederick 'Jack' Perkins of 73 Squadron. had to make an instant decision.

Pilot sergeant Jack Perkins.

The extraordinary thing, he recalled later, was that the morning he was shot down was the only time in his life that anybody needed to remind him – as his fitter did then – about a vital piece of his equipment.

'I looked down, and to my surprise I'd forgotten to put the parachute leg straps through the loops and into the central buckle. If I hadn't, I would have slipped right through the parachute when I had to bale out.

'When we took off, I took my position in the leading section on the right of Flying Officer Smith, who was leading the squadron. We climbed to 20,000 feet over the Chelmsford area. We were told over the radio that 20 escorted bandits were approaching the east coast at 20,000 feet, and so we patrolled over there but didn't see anything. About five minutes later we were told to descend to 5,000 feet, where 50 escorted Jerries were said to be approaching the coast. We dived down and almost immediately were ordered back to 20,000 feet, where masses of enemy fighters were said to be.

I could almost hear Smithy swearing at our having lost height for no reason, but we started up again and steadily climbed towards London. We had almost reached 20,000 feet, the sky was perfectly clear and the sun was shining brightly . . . Suddenly there was an almighty explosion and the whole of my cockpit was enveloped in flames. A petrol flame is far more intense, hotter and fiercer than almost any other type of fire I know of. In the Hurricane, you had a reserve tank of petrol right in front of you, in between the engine and the cockpit. You had that straight in the face. The only thing in your mind is that you must get out of this. People who stayed in a burning cockpit for ten seconds were overcome by the flames and the heat. Nine seconds and you ended up in Queen Victoria Hospital at East Grinstead in Dr. Archie McIndoe's burns surgery for the rest of the war. However, if you got out in eight seconds, you never flew again, but you went back about 12 times for plastic surgery.

'I reckon that, undoing my straps, I got out of that burning 'plane in four or five seconds. I thought that in my hurry I had kicked off my parachute at the same time. With the flames all around me, I didn't care. I had got out of the plane, but found myself held in place by my oxygen lead as well as my radio lead, both of which were still attached to my flying helmet and to the inside of the cockpit. I was actually going down with the plane, but outside of it. It was spiralling down in flames and I was on the outside but by the side of the cockpit, my legs towards the tail.

'As we gathered speed, still spiralling down, my helmet was wrenched off my head. I fell free. I had this lovely feeling of cool air, I was away from the burning and crashing aircraft. I thought, "This must be heaven". I just let myself fall, there was nothing else to do, there was nothing else I wanted to do. I thought I was falling to my death, with my parachute kicked off, but at that stage I didn't mind,

---

FLYER BIOG

Sergeant Frederick Stanley 'Jack' Perkins, RAF Service No. 104446 of 73 Squadron, was based at Church Fenton.

He was flying Hurricane No. V7445 and shot down over Sheppey about 11am on Monday 23rd September 1940, almost certainly by a Me 109 of JG26. The aircraft crashed in the Swale, Emley. Perkins suffered only slight injuries, was quickly patched up and was soon back flying again.

He joined 421 Flight at Gravesend on 25th October 1940. This was later expanded and strengthened to squadron status and renumbered 91 Squadron (Nigeria) in January 1941 and based at Hawkinge. He was commissioned in August 1941 and two years later was promoted to flight lieutenant.

During the early months of January 1944 he was posted to Hythe, Kent, where he was directing the fight by Spitfires and Tempests in intercepting the VI Flying Bombs.

He was released from the RAF in May 1946 as a flight lieutenant. He died in 1988.

91 (Nigeria) Squadron. Jack Perkins is fourth from the left.

I was just so glad to be away from the flames and I was dazed by the shock of one instant being in close formation with my leader and the next instant being in a fiercely burning cockpit.

'The lovely cool air was just marvellous, wonderful. I just continued to fall. Then I began to feel sick, horribly sick. I later turned out not to be badly burnt, but at the time there was a nasty smell of burning flesh and burning hair. I realised I was somersaulting; I saw the ground and then the sky and then the ground and then the sky. I thought "I can't stand this any longer" and then, "I wish I still had my parachute". I reached for the ring as a matter of routine, and there it was, I felt for the pack and that was also there, on my back, I hadn't kicked it off after all. I pulled the ring and there was an enormous jerk on my crotch as the main 'chute opened and I was pulled up at speed. 'The feeling was not of relief or exaltation – just surprise, total surprise."

Waring's Escape

Winston Churchill and a few government officials visited RAF Kenley during the Battle of Britain, on the 24th August 1940. He was anxious to meet the young fighter pilots who were based there. A new squadron had just been posted in to Kenley – 616 Squadron, which had arrived a few days previously.

Sgt. Philip Waring
[P. Cartwright]

One of these pilots was Sgt. Phil Waring, one of the older pilots in the squadron who was then just coming up to his 25th birthday.

'Churchill visited Kenley Aerodrome five days after we got there,' he recalled. 'We were scrambled soon after he arrived. I was in 'B' flight and took off in Spitfire No. K 9819. I thought it was something put on just for his benefit, but we intercepted some Germans near Canterbury – fighters on top, bombers underneath. 'A' Flight went for the bombers. We went for the fighters, which had formed a defensive ring. We just barged in. It was an unholy melée. The sky was full of aircraft, all very close and going in all directions. I saw four Germans in a line astern going off to France and went after them. I pressed the emergency boost to get double power. I caught up with them over the Channel and fired at each one in turn. I thought, "This is easy".

'I could see my tracer bullets hitting or appearing to hit them. Down they went with smoke coming out, and I thought, "I'm going to be an Ace; four already, all at once". Not until later did I learn that the Germans' way of getting out of a jam was to turn upside down and put full boost on. A lot of smoke comes out of them as they dive away – and that may be what happened, though I've always thought I really got at least one of those for sure and probably damaged the others.

'But my aircraft must have been hit in the radiator during the earlier melée, because after I intercepted the four Germans over the Channel it started to get hot. The oil pressure and temperature went right off the clock. I didn't realise it, but I was now over France; it took only three minutes to fly across the Channel. I was beginning to slow down and another lot of Germans appeared and went for me. I was getting slower and slower and then my engine caught fire. I side-slipped and it went out; I was almost gliding by then.

'The Germans were using me for target practice. Their machine-gun bullets on my armour plating sounded like one of those old alarm clocks going off. My aircraft was very badly hit. I did a very steep turn to get away and spun down a couple of thousand feet. That shook them off for a minute or so, though it may have only been seconds. I had no idea of time: I thought the whole thing lasted an hour, but it probably was only 10 minutes.

FLYER BIOG

Philip Thomas Waring was born in 1915 and educated at Bishop Vesey's Grammar School at Sutton Coldfield. He joined the RAF in May 1939 as an airman u/t pilot and was called to full time service on 1st September. He completed his flying training and joined 616 Squadron at Leconfield in June 1940.

After capture, he spent time in several prisoner of war camps, and on the 18th April 1941 he was transferred to Stalag Luft III at Sagan. In September he volunteered to go as an orderly with a group of officers who were being sent to Oflag XXIB, Schubin, as a punishment for their escape activities. Orderlies were allowed out to Schubin railway station to collect parcels, rations and coal, with only a few guards. On his third outing, on the 16th December 1942, he slipped away. Two days later he reached Graudenz hoping to board a ship, but he was unlucky. He then made his way to Danzig and managed to board a Swedish ship that was being loaded with coal. The ship was searched by the Germans before it left, but Wareing was not found. He was discovered by crew members on the 23rd and they kept him hidden, feeding him with bread and water. The captain found out, and as they docked he handed him over to the police. The British Consul was informed,and on the 28th he was in their hands, safe at last.

On the 5th January he flew out, landing at Leuchars. He was taken to the War Office for debriefing and later spent several months lecturing. He was commissioned from a warrant officer in July 1943 and was awarded the DCM on 14th December 1943. He spent the rest of the war as an instructor and was discharged from the RAF in late 1945 with the rank of flight lieutenant. He died in May 1987.

'I looked at my poor Spitfire. It was a new one and I'd only had it a few days – now there were holes all over it. I knew I had to get out. There was a lot of smoke. It seemed to go quiet again for a moment. I opened the cockpit lid, undid my straps and took off my helmet. I thought I had remembered everything that I had to do. I was going to turn upside down to fall out, when I was hit again, a cannon shell I think, and then everything happened at once.

'The petrol tanks just in front of me went up in flames. I felt the heat coming up my legs. At the same time they blew my tail off and I was thrown clear of the plane. I'd heard stories that the Germans might shoot at you when you were parachuting down, so I delayed pulling the ripcord.

'I was thrown out of the plane at 6,000 feet but didn't open my parachute till I was down to about 1,000 feet. I was tumbling over and over, waiting until the Messerschmitts got smaller and smaller in the distance so they wouldn't get at me. The ground came up very quickly. When I opened my parachute it was only a matter of seconds before I landed, but it was an easy landing anyway.

'I came down in a field near the Channel coast in France [near Calais-Marck airfield]. A German motorcycle with a sidecar came riding up to me. The driver drew his pistol and pointed at me and said "Haben sie pistol?" I said, "Don't be silly." He spoke a little English and said, "For you, the war is over." I think they all said things like that. He put his pistol away, put me in the sidecar and with another chap riding behind him, took me to an airfield close by.

'I was very impressed with that field. The planes and everything there were very well camouflaged, far better than ours were. It was haymaking time and the aircraft were literally under the hay, well hidden.

'The Germans were very friendly; of course they were winning, or thought they were. One chap said to me, "Cheer up, we'll be in London next week and you will soon be home." They had quite a party for me. They said that they were sorry they'd finished all the English whisky that they had captured at Dunkirk and they only had French brandy and beer. It was good fun, really. Some of them showed me family photographs. Two of them asked for my home address, and one of them was shot down over England a few days later – either with my address in his pocket or he said during interrogation that he'd seen me. That was the first news anyone at home had that I was still alive.

'They took off early next morning. I watched them form up above. It was very impressive – several hundred aircraft going round and round, getting into their massive formations. I was then taken away and spent a day in the office of an adjutant. He was writing letters of condolence to families of Germans who were being shot down. He told me, "Not only you, we lose a lot too."

'I ended up in a prison camp in Germany, where I was interrogated. They asked a lot of innocuous questions, pretending it was routine. One German asked, "How is it that you're always there when we come?" I said, "We have powerful binoculars and watch all the time." They didn't query that at all.'

Allan Wright's Story

Allan Wright was born in Teignmouth, Devon on 12 February 1920. At the age of 18 he attended the RAF College at Cranwell, with the intention of gaining a permanent commission in the RAF. On the 29th October 1939 he was commissioned and posted to Tangmere, as a pilot officer to join the newly reforming 92 Squadron. The Squadron was being equipped with Blenheim IVs for night fighting. The problem at this time was that there were no guns or radios ready for them, which meant that they were useless for night fighting. The squadron was re-equipped with Spitfires during March and was then posted to Northolt. During the Dunkirk operations the squadron flew from Duxford, Hornchurch and Martlesham Heath.

Wg.-Cmdr. Allan Wright. [A. Wright]

Wright experienced plenty of action over Dunkirk. On the 23rd May he shot down a Me110 and damaged another, while a third he was credited as a 'possible.' The following day he was credited with a Heinkel He111 as a 'possible' – and he was still only 20 years of age. On the 2nd June he shot down his first Me109, over Dunkirk. His Spitfire no. N 3250 'S' had suffered 16 bullet strikes and was replaced by R 6596, his code letter 'S' being transferred to this aircraft and later to every subsequent replacement.

About the middle of June 1940, after the Dunkirk operation, the squadron was posted to Pembury in South Wales. About 11pm on Thursday 29th August 1940, while flying Spitfire no. R6596 on a night patrol, he attacked a Heinkel He111H of NO. 3/KG27 in the Bristol area. This aircraft was flown by Oberleutnant Huenerbein and had a crew of four, all of whom baled out after their aircraft was attacked. They landed, incurring various degrees of injury. One crew member, Obergerfreiter Walpert, later died of the injuries he suffered. The pilot and the other crew members, Unteroffiziers Schlosser and Siebers, became prisoners of war..

The Heinkel was shot down on one of the very few successful Spitfire 'cats-eye' patrols, and said a lot for the flying skill of Pilot Officer Allan Wright at this stage of the war. The German bomber jettisoned its bombs over fields on the Wiltshire/Hampshire border. As the aircraft came down at a fast speed, it skimmed the rooftops of the villages at North Charford and Hatchet Green. It then struck a large oak tree and high tension cables which turned it in flight, bringing it down on a house in the village of Hale, where it came to rest in the back garden. A young boy, John Alexander, had a very lucky escape when he was trapped in the house when the ceiling collapsed and fell on his bed. He was rescued unhurt although rather frightened.

On the 8th September, and at only 24 hours' notice, the squadron was again moved, this time to Biggin Hill. On his first sortie the next day Allan Wright shot at one Me109E but in the process was 'bounced' by another. His gun sight in front of his face was destroyed by one of 17 bullets that hit his Spitfire, and he could no longer take part in the dogfight. Spitfire X4069 now became 'S.' Thereafter he was in action sometimes flying three sorties a day, as Hitler started the

Heinkel He111 shot down by Allan Wright in the Bristol area on 29th August 1940. [W. Hargreaves]

blitz of London. On the 27th September he was promoted to 'B' Flight Commander. During this short time at Biggin Hill he was involved in combat with a large number of German raiders. On the 11th he shot down a Heinkel He111 over East London and a 'probable' Me109 over Folkestone, then had 'probables' and a 'damaged' over Tunbridge Wells, Canterbury and Dover. On the 26th he shot down a Dornier over Tenterden. His best day of combat was probably on the 27th when in two actions over Sevenoaks, Kent, he shot down a Junkers Ju88, had a half share in a Heinkel He111, damaged a Dornier and then damaged two Junkers Ju88s. This was certainly a day he would remember.

On the 30th September he was again in action. He shot down a Me109E near Redhill and later found himself near the south coast. About 5pm he seriously damaged another Me109E over Redhill. Being out of ammunition he followed it down until it crashed into the sea south of Newhaven. However, on his return across the sea he was 'bounced' by a Me109 flown by Lieutenant Wiesinger of No. 4/JG27, based at Cherbourg, as he was flying westwards towards Brighton. His Spitfire was badly shot up and damaged, and he was wounded in his right thigh and buttocks by cannon shell splinters. Despite the damage, he managed to shake off the enemy fighter by a series of tight turns.

Because of the damage, his Spitfire was difficult to control and keep on a steady course. He became aware that the blood from his wound was squelching in his boot. He reached the coast near Brighton and turned west looking for a sizeable field to get his Spitfire onto the ground. He knew it would be too difficult for him to clear the cockpit if he tried to bale out. Shoreham soon appeared and he was relieved to get his plane down without mishap. Having heaved himself out of the cockpit he looked back in amazement at the state of the fuselage. The tail was in tatters, the metal skin of the fuselage peppered with cannon shell splinters and the belly of it half way to the cockpit slit open as if with a can opener. The propeller had bullet holes too. Only the engine, fortunately, had been untouched. The airfield was practically deserted.

Two dishevelled airmen helped him into their own little two-seater car. There was an ambulance on the tarmac, but its crew were in the hanger unaware that they were needed. They helped him get in, but the engine wouldn't start. He commandeered a passing ancient RAF lorry and ordered the driver to take him to the nearest hospital, which was Southlands in Southwick, near Shoreham.

What a disorganised place! Trying not to pass out, he found himself clasping the hand of one of the airmen. Arriving at the hospital, he found that the enemy raid he had been battling with had caused casualties which were already being received there, so his stretcher was set aside. This was the last straw. Nothing was going to happen unless he made it happen. He shouted out until someone came over, slit his trouser leg and had a look at the damage. As he was coming round, after the pieces of shrapnel had been extracted from his leg, thigh, buttocks and elbow, he heard cheerful voices asking about his love life – what little there was of it – and being answered. The cheeky things knew a body in these circumstances had no mental resistance. There were two in the ward he had been

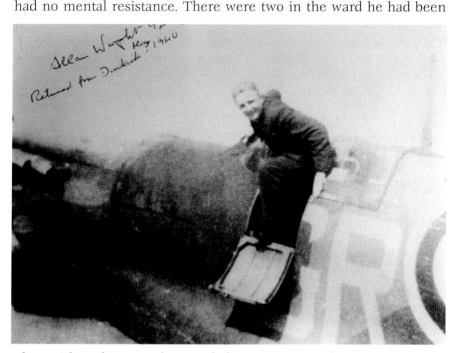

Alan Wright on his return from Dunkirk in 1940. [A. Wright]

FLYER BIOGS

It would be remiss not to mention a little more about three other members of 92 Squadron:

Jamie Rankin was born in Edinburgh on 7th May 1913, joined the RAF and was commissioned in 1935. During his service he flew with 64 and 92 Squadrons, as well as with the Biggin Hill Wing. He was a flight lieutenant in June 1940 and a brilliant Spitfire pilot. His total kills for the war period amounted to 17 destroyed (another 5 shared), 3 probables (2 others shared) 16 damaged (3 shared) and 1 destroyed on water.

He was promoted to air commodore in 1945 but reverted to group captain when the war ended. In 1954 he commanded RAF Duxford, and with 'Johnnie' Johnson and Peter Thompson flew one of the last three Spitfires in RAF service on their final service flight. He retired from the RAF in November 1958, returning to Edinburgh, where he died some years later.

Desmond Gordon (Bill) Williams was also a brilliant Spitfire pilot, and even with his untimely death 10th October 1940 he was classed as an Ace. At the time of his death he had shot down 5 enemy aircraft and another shared, 2 unconfirmed destroyed, 2 probables and 6 damaged.

He was killed, having collided with FO Drummond while attacking a Dornier over Tangmere. His Spitfire X4038 crashed in Fallowfield Crescent, Hove at 8.15am. Flying Officer Drummond, flying Spitfire R6616, was wounded in the leg and arm. He managed to bale out but too low, and he was killed. His Spitfire crashed and burned out in Jubilee Field, Portslade.

John Fraser Drummond is the third of my three 92 Squadron stars. He joined the RAF on a short commission in April 1938, going first to 46 Squadron in January 1939. Late in May 1940 he went with his unit to Northern Norway and saw action over the Narvik area after flying his Hurricane from the deck of HMS Glorious. When the area was evacuated he returned to the United Kingdom. At this time HMS Glorious was sunk and some members of the Squadron were lost. He was awarded the DFC in July for his part in the campaign. He was posted to 92 Squadron in September, taking part in the final month of the Battle of Britain. Then on 10th October while attacking a Do 17 together with Bill Williams, both Spitfires collided in a horrific accident and he lost his life. He was aged just 21. His short wartime tally was 8, and 1 shared ,destroyed, 3 probables and 4 damaged. Had he lived I am sure he too would have been an Ace.

put in, and later on these nurse 'creatures' would, while they were out of their ward, sew up their pyjama legs for a joke. The idea was to surprise them in their nakedness. They wondered how they could get their own back, and the only thing they could think of was to lace their tea with a laxative.

One night the Germans bombed the town. The nurses rushed in: 'Under the bed, under the bed!' They hesitated, false bravado really, but the bombs were falling, brilliantly flashing outside the windows, which were rattling hard enough for a near hit to bring the glass crashing down into the room. They soon thought better of their bravery. After all, he thought, what was the point of getting so far, only to be killed in bed?

He was in Southlands Hospital for about ten days. It would be nearly two months before he was back flying with 92 squadron, because his wounds took a long time to heal properly. His second stripe had been lost to Bob Holland who had taken over 'B' Flight.

The squadron had made further gains and had also suffered a number of losses, including his good friend Bill Williams, who had flown with him so often. Bill had been sent off in a section of three to intercept a single Dornier. The enemy aircraft was desperately trying to hide, flying through patches of broken cloud. When it appeared through a gap, he and Drummond, another of the three, had launched themselves at it, from either side in quarter attacks, but as their aircraft slid in from either side in behind the Dornier, neither could see each other and they collided. Two good pilots were lost without having achieved any success.

'While I was in hospital, a small un-addressed envelope was handed to me, containing several small photographs of my much-damaged Spitfire at the edge of the airfield. There was nothing to show who had sent them. A very kind thought.'

On the 22nd October he was told that he had been awarded the DFC and returned to his squadron operations in November. He was rested in July 1941 after having destroyed four more Me109's and damaging another. He was awarded a Bar to his DFC at this time.

It is interesting to note that the next Me109 shot down after Newhaven was the 20th enemy aircraft he had either shot down or damaged – at the age of 20. He certainly was a real Ace.

In October 1942, together with Jamie Rankin, he was in the USA training the USAAF Squadrons in tactics and gunnery. He joined 29 night fighter squadron flying Beaufighters in March 1943 as 'A' Flight commander. He shot down a Junkers Ju88 which was mine-lying at a very low level over the sea, and he damaged another on 3rd April. He was promoted to wing commander in December to command the Air Fighting Development Unit, and was awarded the AFC in September for his work there. In February 1945 he was posted to Egypt to command the Middle East Advanced Bombing and Gunnery School at El Ballah and then to command the base for a short time. He had a number of appointments over the next years, including HQ Middle East, the Air Ministry and a spell at the RAF College Cranwell, where it all started – this time as a lecturer.

He flew many of the post-war jet aircraft, mostly Hunters and Javelins. In March 1960, he was appointed Group Captain Plans, Far East Air Force, followed in 1962 by two years at HQ Fighter Command. Finally, in late 1964 he was in command of the ballistic missile early warning station – the famous 'giant golf balls' – on the Yorkshire Moors at Fylingdales, near Whitby. He retired in February 1967 and went to live in the west country, ending a spectacular career in the Royal Air Force.

The Death of a Dornier

This is the story of the demise of an attacking Dornier Do 17Z on Battle of Britain day, 15th September 1940. It was attacked at about 12.40pm over the Kent countryside. The pilot, Oberfeldwebel Niebler, was conscious of the fact that staying in formation was the safest way against an attack by British fighters.

His was one of 25 Dornier bombers of KG76, based at Cormeilles-en-Vexin, France. On this day they had been briefed to attack the railway viaducts at Battersea. The area was one of the busiest parts of the railways to the south of London and was the hub of the Southern Railway, which covered all parts of the south of England.

As the formation was flying over Kent, together with their escorts, they were attacked by numerous Spitfires and Hurricanes, as almost all of the Squadrons in 11 Group were airborne and had been positioned between the Channel and London, awaiting the arrival of the enemy bombers.

Low-level flying Dornier DO 17s, known as 'flying pencils'.

Pilot Officer Jim Meaker of 249 Squadron 'B' Flight, based at North Weald, was trying to get his Hurricane among the bombers. He selected Dornier no. 2651 flown by Niebler and, finger poised over the button, patiently waited for his opportunity. He fired off a three-second burst, striking the bomber so that the port engine came to a visible stop. The pilot took evading action, diving away from the Hurricane, and Meaker concentrated on the starboard engine.

'I attacked one on the edge of the formation,' he wrote in his diary. 'Get him straight away and he leaves the rest of his boys. Follow him, plugging all the time. A quarter attack comes off beautifully; see bullets going in, in a line from the nose back to the tail, at intervals of a foot all the way down. See the rear gunner lying in his seat, probably dead. Dornier is smoking like a chimney, can smell it from behind him. Oil comes back on my aircraft and pieces fly past me. Then three blasted Spitfires horn in and drive me away from my own

---

FLYER BIOG

James Reginald Bryan Meaker was born on 19th January 1919 in Kinsale, Co. Cork.

He joined the RAF on a short service commission on 26th June 1939. He attended various training courses and was posted to 12 Group pool, Aston Down, on 24th February 1940 to convert to Hurricanes. On 31st March he joined 46 Squadron at Digby. He was there but a short while before being posted to 263 Squadron at Scapa Flow on 4th May. The Squadron's Gladiators were loaded on to HMS Furious, which sailed for Norway on 14th May and were unloaded a week later. The Squadron were withdrawn on 7th June and Meaker returned to England by sea.

He then joined 249 Squadron at Leconfield in late June and soon opened his account of destroying enemy aircraft. His first victim was a Me110 which he shot down on 15th August in the Ringwood area of Hampshire. In total he claimed 7 destroyed, 2 shared, 1 probable and at least 2 damaged.

About 3.30pm on the 27th September 1940 he shared in the destruction of a Me110, but his aircraft was hit by crossfire from a formation of five Junkers Ju88s and shot down. He managed to bale out but hit the tail plane of his Hurricane and fell to his death at Warren Field, Brightling Park. His Hurricane no. P3834 crashed at Brake Field, Giffords Farm, Dallington. In 1990 a memorial was placed near the spot where he was killed.

He was awarded the DFC on 8th October 1940. He is buried in West Dean Cemetery, West Sussex.

private and personal Dornier. One guy bales out from the Jerry. He has his arms folded and seems quite resigned. His ship crashes in flames and Spitfires shoot a line all around it . . .

'They're getting quite a reputation for pinching a bomber when a Hurricane has got it on the run. So I go home first and claim it before they can.'

Oberleutnant Karl-Ernst Wilkie, the navigator in the Dornier, takes up the story: 'The gunner, Unteroflizier Schatz was the first to be killed. His job was to operate the guns each side of the cabin, to provide defence against fighter attacks from the left or right. The poor guy was hit during the initial attack. I was hit by a bullet from the right; it struck me in the face, just below my nose and blinded me. From that moment on I took no further part in the action. A fire suddenly broke out in the cabin and the radio operator, Unteroffizier Zremer, suffered severe burns. The Dornier was in a hopeless position; the pilot knew it and ordered us to bale out.

'Slowly, the radio operator crawled along the floor to the escape hatch. He struggled with it for a few seconds, released it and jumped, I followed him out.'

The three Spitfires were flown by Flt. Lt. Gillies and PO Bodie of 66 Squadron and PO Pollard of 611 Squadron. All three pilots fired long bursts into the crippled bomber. Bodie saw the two crewmen bale out of the aircraft. He then went in for a closer look.

'The Dornier was pretty well riddled,' he wrote later. 'The machine guns certainly made a mess. I had a look at the pilot, he sat bolt upright in his seat and was either dead or wounded for he didn't turn his head to look at me or watch out for a place to land, but just stared straight ahead. The machine went down, the pilot must have been dead, he made no attempt to flatten out ready to land. It went smack into a field and then the aircraft exploded. I saw the pieces sail past me as I flew low overhead. I didn't feel particularly jubilant.'

The Dornier crashed north of Sturry, about four miles east of Canterbury, close to the A28 Canterbury to Margate road. Wilkie and Zremer were captured on landing, Zremer being admitted to hospital with severe burns. The three other members of the crew (Oberfeldwebel Niebler, Feldwebel Wiseman and Unteroffizier Schatz) were killed.

The Last Day Raids

On Monday, 30th September 1940 the Luftwaffe returned to heavy day attacks. Fighter Command was ready for them, however, and the bombers were repulsed with very heavy losses. These proved to be the Kampfgeschwader's last large-scale day raids on England.

In attempting to defend their bombers, German fighters suffered a humiliating and heavy defeat. The full extent of it is measured by the fact that more than 25 Messerschmitt Me109s were lost, while a number of others crash-landed in France.

One of the Jagdgeschwaders taking part on this day was J.G.26. For them, it was one of their worst days of the Battle of Britain, losing four pilots and making only seven victory claims.

The German fighter pilots claimed the shooting down of five Hurricanes without loss. In fact two Hurricanes were destroyed and the other three made forced landings: the aircraft, though damaged, were deemed repairable. One pilot, FO Malcolm Ravenhill, was killed and two others were slightly wounded.

The Jagdgeschwader's brilliant commander, Major Adolph Galland, led three escort missions on this day – one in the morning, when soon after 10.30am the second Gruppe met the Hurricanes of No. 229 Squadron, based at Northolt, over Tonbridge in Kent. An early afternoon mission was flown without incident, but there were a number of problems on the evening mission.

About 5pm, they were acting as escort to KG 77 on a bombing mission to London. As they arrived just south of the capital they encountered Hurricanes of 303 (Polish) Squadron who attempted to drive away the escort from the German bombers.

Major Galland's wing-man, Hptm. Walter Kienzle was shot down but, although badly injured, managed to bale out. He landed safely in the Rochester area and saw out the rest of the war as a POW. Galland, the leader, then attacked a lone Hurricane, which blew up, covering his canopy with oil. The RAF pilot was Sergeant Marian Belc, of 303 (Polish) Squadron. He managed to bale out, suffering no injuries, south of Guildford. This was Major Galland's 42nd victory of the war.

Me109 pilot Horst Perez, shot down 30th September on the downs at East Dean, near Eastbourne. [J. Widgeon]

Oblt. Walter Horten, another of the German pilots in this battle, claimed the shooting down of two Hurricanes of 303 Squadron, but there is only the one aircraft loss on record – that shot down by Galland. The rest of the Geschwader claimed no victories.

On their way home, the 4th.Staffel's Uffz. Horst Perez was in combat with a Spitfire from 92 Squadron. He managed to force land his Me.109E-4 No. 1190 (white 4) about 5.30pm at East Dean, near Eastbourne, just south of the A259. He was captured and became a prisoner of war.

Two other German JG26 pilots, Fw. Konrad Carl and Gefr. Helmut Hornatschek, found themselves intercepted by a squadron of Spitfires. Carl was attacked as he left the Sussex shores near Beachy Head. He was flying his Me.109E –4 No. 3891 and was badly shot up but somehow managed to cross the Channel and effect a bad landing at his French base, Caffiers. He was taken to hospital with a number of injuries. Helmet Hornatschek, flying Me.109E-1 No.4820, was less fortunate. He was shot down over the Thames Estuary and lost his life.

John Beard's Story

John Maurice Bentley Beard was born on 20th December 1918 at Shoreham, West Sussex. He attended Leamington College and on completion of his education went into banking. He was working for the Midland Bank in Leamington Spa when he joined the RAFVR in June 1937.

John Beard.

He began his weekend flying at 9 E&RFTS, Ansty and trained on Avro Cadets and Hawker Harts. He was called up on 2nd September 1939. He was posted to 2 FTS, Brize Norton, on 7th October and from there joined 600 Squadron at Drem on 15th December.

On 16th May 1940 he was posted to 249 Squadron when it was re-formed at Church Fenton.

At 6pm on Saturday the 7th September he was shot down when the squadron was in combat with Dornier Do 17s over the north east of London. His Hurricane, no. N 2440, was believed to have been hit by 'friendly' AA fire.

During this engagement, six squadron Hurricanes were shot down, three pilots being wounded and one killed: PO Robert Fleming baled out on fire and died later from burns and shock.

During September and October he enjoyed success when he destroyed a Dornier Do 17 near Rochford, Essex, and he followed it up four days later when he destroyed a Me.109E in the same area.

On the 18th he destroyed a Me110 and on the 27th, his best day, he destroyed two Me109s 10 miles east of Ramsgate, a Me110 and another one as a probable, as well as a Dornier Do 17, also near Redhill.

He takes up the story, as flying as Red 3,he sighted a lone Dornier Do 17 near Canterbury at 15.15 hours.

'I became separated from the squadron, and near Canterbury saw a bomber heading east. I caught it about seven miles out to sea and fired three short bursts; some brown smoke came from the port engine. It began to lose height. I saw a fighter in my mirror and turned sharply to get behind it. It took little evasive action and my second burst . . . sent it into the sea. I then followed another Me109 near me, turning towards my tail. I had a dogfight with him and after some time fired a burst from the quarter. The machine caught fire and went into the sea. I did not see the bomber again.'

On the 28th he destroyed a Me109 in the Dover area, the German pilot being Hptm. Rolf Pingel, who was the Staffelkapitan of 2/JG26. He survived the ditching and was rescued by Luftwaffe's Seenotflugkommando. (He was less lucky in a later sortie in July 1941, when he was shot down over Kent and spent the rest of the war as a POW.)

On the 12th October Beard damaged a Me109E, again in the Dover area. He was awarded the DFM on the 22nd October.

On the 25th October while flying Hurricane No. P 3615, he was involved in combat and was shot down by a Me109. He baled out over north Kent, wounded, and was admitted to Pembury Hospital. His aircraft is believed to have crashed at Rankin's Farm, Linton.

He was commissioned on 18th December and posted to 52 OTU at Debden on 30th April 1941. He moved to the CGS at Sutton Bridge on March 18th 1942 as a founder member of the pilot gunnery wing there and took charge of the live firing flight. The PGW later moved to Catfoss, to become part of the control gunnery school.

He became a member of the Fighter Command Test Board and made a number of visits to the Gunnery Research Unit at Exeter to carry out tests on new pieces of armament equipment.

John Beard was promoted to flying officer on 18th December 1941 and to flight lieutenant a year later. He was awarded the AFC on the 1st January 1945. His last job was to arrange the return of 120 lease lend expeditors to the Americans in Munich in early 1946. He flew the last one back himself and was discharged from the RAF as a squadron leader on reaching the UK.

His hobby had become electronics, and after working in his father-in-law's shop, he decided to set up as an electronic engineer, making specialist test equipment for the motor industry.

A Special Kind of Bravery

Sergeant David Cox was one of those rare young men whose first thought was for others. He hated anything that he deemed as being unfair and was never slow in coming forward to make his point. He was 20 years old at the time of the Battle of Britain and, although young, was blessed with a maturity far in excess of his tender age. This is a small part of his life and indicates his thoughts for other people – although, sadly, on this occasion, his advice was not heeded in time.

'There was one sergeant, Jack Roden, who should never have been a fighter pilot,' he said later. 'He was one of the bravest men I ever knew. He was dead scared from the beginning, but he kept on flying.

'I used to say to him, "Go to the C. or to your flight commander and get taken off". He wouldn't. He used to crash Spitfires in all sorts of silly ways – three or four of them. He was frightened of the plane. He never shot anything down.

'One day, he got shot up and badly hurt trying to land his damaged Spitfire in a field. If he had crash-landed with his wheels up he'd have been all right. He'd have come to a grinding halt quickly but landed with his wheels down. The field was too small, and he ran into a tree and was badly injured. He was conscious at first, to be asked why the heck he had put his wheels down when he could have crash-landed it. He said that it was because he didn't want to damage another Spitfire. He died three days later. It was so unnecessary; he should never have been a fighter pilot.'

He spoke later about pilots in general and the limited time allowed for their training because of a shortage of pilots during and just after the Battle of Britain in the summer and autumn of 1940.

'There were others who were ill placed. It was inevitable. We were so short of pilots and there were a few who didn't want to be there. The one who was easiest to spot was the one who always came back with something wrong with his aircraft – the radio had gone or the revs were dropping or it wasn't flying right or it was overheating. If it happened often, the flight commander or CO would say, "The next

FLYER BIOG

David Cox was born on 18th April 1920 at Cambridge, but went to school in Bournemouth. His first job was to work as a clerk in a solicitor's office. He failed a medical to join the RAF and worked for some months at Billingsgate Market in an effort to build himself up. He joined the RAFVR in April 1939 as an airman trainee pilot. He completed his training and was posted to 19 Squadron at Duxford on the 23rd May 1940.

He flew as part of the 'Bader' wing and in early September he shot down a Me109 over Maidstone. His own Spitfire was badly damaged during the dogfight, and it was all he could do to limp back to base. As he landed, Bader himself was there and told him that his aircraft was a 'bloody mess'. In his defence he pointed out that he had shot down a Me 109. That meant nothing to Bader, who snapped at him that a 'one-for-one ratio was not so f.....g good.'

Early one Monday morning (August 19th) he was just getting out of bed when the squadron were scrambled. He had no option but to wear his flying gear over his pyjamas, but he still managed to share in the destruction of a Me 110.

His part in the Battle of Britain ended abruptly on Friday 27th September, when German fighters jumped his formation. He went to the aid of a comrade, PO Eric Burgoyne, and they were both shot down. Burgoyne was killed, but Cox baled out, wounded by shrapnel and with fragments in his legs. He spent three months in hospital, and it would be almost five months before he returned to active duty. He was awarded a DFC and bar.

He had a distinguished wartime career receiving a commission in July 1941. He was promoted to flight lieutenant on 17th July 1943. He was rewarded with the command of 222 Squadron. Equipped with Spitfire IX's he was involved with patrols over the Normandy landings on the 6th June 1944. He was awarded the Croix de Guerre avec Palme for his work over this period.

Soon after D-Day and with the Allies advancing across France, Cox was involved in a serious car crash, which put paid to his career for a while. He returned in January 1945 and took command of No.1 Squadron, flying Spitfires on long-range bomber escorts. Three months later, in April he was promoted to wing commander and left for Burma. His wing of two Spitfire squadrons supported the 14th army's advance to Rangoon and remained there until the last day of the war against Japan in August 1945.

Married in 1939, he retired from the RAF in March 1946. He died on 20th January 2004.

time it happens, have it tested on the ground or have someone else take it right up again." If the plane was found to be all right, the pilot would be posted away.'

FLYER BIOG

Sgt Henry Adrian Roden was born in Bradford in August 1916 and was educated at Bellahouston Academy, Glasgow. He joined the RAFVR in July 1937. He was called up on 1st September 1939 and after training he was posted to 19 Squadron at Duxford on 6th May 1940.

On the 28th July he crashed on landing at Duxford after an attack on a Junkers Ju88. He was unhurt. Four days later he made a crash-landing in Spitfire No. P 9431 after his glycol tank was damaged in action against Me 109's. He suffered slight injuries and the aircraft was written off.

Following action against Me110's off Harwich on 15th November 1940 he hit a tree while attempting a forced landing in bad visibility in Spitfire P 7420. He later died from the injuries he sustained, and is buried in Linithgow Cemetery, West Lothian.

The Sick Spitfire

On Sunday 18th August 1940, 602 Squadron was called into combat as a large German force had been sent to attack Tangmere airfield. The pilots ran to their Spitfires to get airborne but when Flt. Lt. Dunlop Urie reached his he found that it was without its wheels because it was being serviced. He immediately ran to another Spitfire (no. X4110) which had been delivered to Westhampnett earlier in the day – a brand new aircraft.

Dunlop Urie now lives in Australia. The following, is a copy from his official report, which he sent to me in his own hand writing.

'We had been at Westhampnett about a week and had been on "readiness" most of the time, from 05.30hrs to 21.00hrs each day – ready to get the squadron into the air at five minutes notice. On 18th August we at last got a long awaited "release", which meant we were not liable for duty, except at two hours notice.

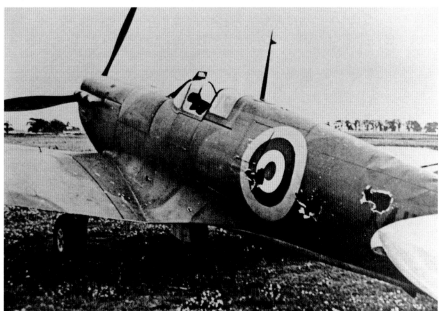

Dunlop Urie's Spitfire no. X4110 at Westhampnett after it had been hit by canon shells on August 18th 1940.

Dunlop Urie at Westhampnett.
[D. Urie]

'We went over to the lovely house which was our mess and sat down to lunch with a pint of beer at our side. I had taken two swallows of this when the phone went. Could we take off as soon as possible, all the Tangmere squadrons were engaged and there was a raid which seemed to be coming for Tangmere again.

'We ran the quarter of a mile back to our aircraft. I had been leading the squadron before we were released and automatically assumed I would still be leading. When I got to my aircraft I found its wheels were off. A new aircraft had been delivered that morning. I grabbed my parachute from my own aircraft and ran for the new one. Its guns had not tuned up with the sights but it seemed important to get airborne to lead the squadron. I reckon we were airborne from the mess in about five minutes.

We were up and ordered to patrol Tangmere at 2,000 feet. I think they were still feeling the raid on the 16th. Someone spotted Ju87s dive bombing Ford, a naval aerodrome about five miles east of Tangmere, and with a "Tally Ho" we made for them. There were two wings each of about 24 aircraft. As I dived down after the second wing Findlay Boyd, who was leading 'B' flight, called up on R/T that he would look after the fighters. I must say, I was so incensed with the Ju87s that I hadn't seen the Me109s. The Ju87 had always seemed to me the meanest aircraft the Germans had. They used it as long range artillery to terrorise fleeing civilians in Belgium and France. I decided that shooting them down didn't matter so much as sending them back badly damaged and wounded.

I reached the formation just as it was pulling up having dropped its bombs. I went right through it and fired at the aircraft before I ran out of ammunition. As I was pulling away, having shot at them, the controller called me up to ask if I was engaged. There was a machine on my tail and I didn't look at it carefully enough in my mirror. As I was thinking how to reply to the controller, I thought it was another Spitfire. However, as I began to answer on the R/T; I was disillusioned. There were four loud bangs and I was blasted out of my seat by a Me109. I didn't dare take violent evasive action – anyway I couldn't, until I regained my seat. He had another go and hit me several times again and then pulled off. I thought of baling out but was too low, so I collected myself and returned to Westhampnett. My R/T was destroyed and I had no flaps and – it transpired – no brakes, and both wheels punctured. I came in over the trees to Westhampnett and my guardian angel was watching over me.

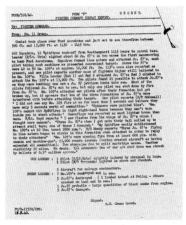

Official 602 Squadron report, signed by intelligence officer O.H. Cranebrook, following the combat during which Dunlop Urie was injured.

We made a good landing and I waited for the ambulance. My legs and parachute were full of shrapnel. Fortunately the fuse of the Me109's cannon shells had been set a fraction too soon and the shells exploded on impact with the skin of the Spitfire. Hector Maclean, who succeeded me in command of 'A' Flight, had a similar experience about a fortnight later. The fuse was more delayed and a shell exploded in his leg.'

The above story is written on four small sheets of paper which are now in the 602 Squadron museum in Glasgow.

Dunlop Urie always admitted that on this day he was the luckiest man alive. During the combat with the enemy aircraft he had taken some 'good hits'. The tail section of the aircraft was badly damaged, with the rudder and aileron cables all but cut through – there was barely a strand holding them together and they could have parted at any moment. His radio had been shot through and was totally dead.

His body was racked with terrible pain. He knew that his legs were badly shot about, but was not sure if he had been hit anywhere else. He thought of taking to his parachute (he later saw that it had been shot to ribbons) but he could not gain any height with his

Dunlop Urie and his wife Mary on their wedding day, 8th September 1939. [D. Urie]

stricken aircraft. There were massive canon shell holes in the fuselage, which made the Spitfire sound like an 'out-of-tune church organ'.

All he knew was that he had to get his aircraft down – safely he hoped. His legs were so painful, with a fiery rasping feel to them, that he thought he would pass out at any moment. He could see his base in the distance and knew he was almost there. He came in low over the trees at Westhampnet, his heart in his mouth.

Now came the test, he thought. Although he managed to get the undercarriage down, the flaps wouldn't move. He got lower and lower and then the he felt the wheels touch the grassy field. The Spitfire bounced and bounced, and each time the pain from his legs shot through his body: he felt every movement the plane made. He had no brakes and he prayed to himself that this agony would soon be over. The aircraft continued its mad dash across the large, uneven field. The ambulance had been alerted and was already racing towards the stricken Spitfire. Eventually, the aircraft came to a stop and, just as it did, the fuselage sagged. Dunlop had landed, but only just. He was gently lifted out of the cockpit and taken to the Royal West Sussex Hospital in Chichester.

However, he wasn't at the hospital very long and returned to the fray within a few days. In December 1940 he was posted to 52 OTU at Aston Down. Later in the war he commanded 151 wing in Russia. He was released from the RAF in 1945 as a wing commander. A year later he re-joined the RauxAF and the re-formed 602 Squadron.

In civilian life he returned to his firm of solicitors with his old colleague, Hector Maclean. He and his wife moved to Helensburgh, where he became a leading light in Clyde yachting circles. He later emigrated to live with his daughter in Australia, where he still is at this time.

Frank Carey's Story

Frank Reginald Carey was born in Brixton, south London on 7th May 1912 and educated at Belvedere School, Haywards Heath, Sussex. He joined the RAF as an apprentice at Halton in September 1927, aged just 15 years. He passed out, having completed the course, in August 1930.

He was posted to 43 Squadron, based at Tangmere, as an AC1 but returned to Halton in 1933 for a conversion course to become an airframes fitter. He was posted to Worthy Down and served with no. 7 and 58 Squadrons until he applied for pilot training in 1935. He laterpassed out as a sergeant pilot from 6 Flight Training School at Netherhaven and rejoined 43 Squadron in September 1936.

Group Captain Frank Carey CBE [Mrs M. Carey]

At the oubreak of war, Frank Carey was still with 43 Squadron and based at Acklington. On Tuesday 30th January 1940 he was involved with his first aerial combat, when he shared in the destruction of a Heinkel He111 while flying his Hurricane L1728. The enemy aircraft crashed into the sea five miles east of Coquet Island, Northumberland, and both the crew and aircraft were lost.

On a particularly cold morning on Saturday 3rd February the squadron was scrambled and shot down three Heinkel He111's, with Frank again taking a share in one of them. The famous Gp/Capt Peter Townsend, also a member of 43 Squadron, later described the action: 'Moments after taking off, I was climbing away from Acklington airfield, Folkes and Sergeant Hallowes in my wake. Vector 190, bandit attacking ship off Whitby. Buster. Our throttles wide-open we raced south at wave-top height, spread out in search formation, Hallowes on my left and Tiger on my right. I searched the low cloud base anxiously. Then suddenly there it was. A Heinkel above and to my right. "Tally ho! two o'clock." There was not a second to lose for the Heinkel was just below the cloud. I banked right in a climbing turn. Now the Heinkel was in my sights. My thumb on the firing button. . . then I was firing at Missy, Wilms, Leuschake and Meyer [the crew]. It never occurred to me that I was killing men, just a big enemy Heinkel.'

In that Heinkel, however, Peter Leuschake was already dead and Johann Meyer, his stomach punctured by bullets, was mortally wounded.

'Closing in fast on the Heinkel I passed it as it entered cloud – a vague black shadow uncomfortably close above. Then Foulkes, the Heinkel and I tumbled out of the cloud almost on top of one another.'

After the Heinkel was forced to land at Bannial Flat Farm in Whitby, special constable Arthur Barratt rushed to the German aircraft and saw the pilot, Feldwebel Wilms burning the official papers. It took five fire extinguishers and several shovels of snow to put the fire out.

Unteroffizer Johann Meyer was screaming in pain. Unteroffizer Peter Leuschake had died instantly, shot through the head and Unteroffizer Karl Missy, the upper gunner, was grievously wounded, with one leg broken and the other terribly mutilated. He cried out in terrible agony as he was dragged clear of the aircraft. Later Peter Townsend visited him in hospital. He had his right leg amputated and was repatriated to Germany in October 1943, in exchange for Allied prisoners of war.

This was the very first enemy aircraft shot down on English soil.

Two other Heinkel's were shot down the same morning with Frank Carey taking a share in one of them. On the 12th February he claimed another Heinkel He111. He was awarded the DFM and commissioned on 1st March. On the 28th he was involved with intercepting yet another He111 east of Wick, sharing ts destruction.

He was posted to no. 3 Squadron, based at Kenley, but was only there for little more than a month as the squadron was sent to France. It was here that he achieved the status of being an Ace pilot. He claimed four He111's and one probable on the day they arrived in France. During the following two days he claimed two more and a probable. However, probably his best day came on 13th May. He shot down two Ju87s and two probable Ju87s, destroyed two He111's, one Dornier Do 17 and had a probable hit on a Me 110. The following day he shot down a Do 17 near Louvain, but his Hurricane was hit by return fire and he was forced to make a crash-landing near Brussels with a leg wound.

Officially it was not known what had happened to him. He was posted as missing in action, and on the 31st May he was awarded the DFC and Bar for his actions. In early June, however, he was evacuated back to England and rejoined 43 Squadron at Tangmere as a flight commander.

In July, as the Battle of Britain started to unfold, he was back in action, and as the month came to a close he claimed one destroyed and three damaged. August came and he continued his onslaught against the enemy, with three destroyed, four probables and three damaged.

On the 18th August, known as 'the 'hardest day', he was leading the squadron into another attack against a raid of Ju87s and Me109s over Thorney Island. During the dogfight he shot down one Ju87 but was shot in the right knee. Trying to return back to base he was ordered not to land at Tangmere because of the raid and was forced to crash-land in a field near Pulborough. He was then admitted to the Royal West Sussex Hospital in Chichester, where he remained until September.

After his recovery he was posted to 52 Operational Training Unit as an instructor, before returning to operations in February 1941 as a flight commander with no. 245 Squadron. He returned to 52 Operational Training Unit, was posted away in July 1941, and then posted yet again, this time to Baginton in August to form and command 135 Squadron. He was then posted to the Far East in Burma during December 1941.

He claimed his first Japanese aircraft on 29th January 1942, shooting down a Nakajima Ki27, over Rangoon. On 12th February he was promoted to wing commander flying of 267 Wing, and he continued to add to his already very impressive combat victories by destroying five more Japanese aircraft during that month. On the 24th March 1942 he was awarded a second Bar to his DFC. His last aerial combat victory occurred on 25th October 1942, when he claimed a probable Nakajima 'Oscar' before being appointed to command RAF Alipore. Later he was posted to Air HQ Bengal, India.

During February, the following year he took command of the air fighting training unit at Amarda Road until November 1944, when he was posted to command 73 OTU at Abu Sueir as a group captain. He remained there until July 1945, when he returned to England, and for his work in India he was awarded the AFC in January 1945.

He was granted a permanent commission and held various staff appointments until 1958, when he was made advisor to the British high commissioner in Australia.

He finally retired from the RAF on the 2nd June 1960, after an impressive career spanning 33 years. He retired as a group captain and was made a CBE on 11th June 1960. He worked for the Rolls Royce aero division in Australia until his retirement, when he returned to live in England. He currently lives in Sussex.

His final score reads 25 and 3 shared destroyed, 4 unconfirmed destroyed, 3 probables, one possible and 8 damaged – and that is some tally!

Ben Bennions – Birth to Death

George Herman 'Ben' Bennions was born in Burslem, Stoke-on-Trent on 15th March 1913. He was besotted with flying and dreamed one day of becoming a pilot or a teacher. (He was eventually to achieve both ambitions.) Still just 16 years of age he joined the RAF Apprentice school at Halton in 1929, graduating as an engineer fitter. A star pupil, he was recommended for the officer cadet college at Cranwell. Although he took basic flying here, however, he did not become a cadet.

Later, he moved to 3 FTS at Grantham to complete his flying training, and in 1935 he was posted to Kharmaksar, Aden, as a Sergeant pilot. He had achieved his aim at the age of just 22 years.

Ben Bennions in 1940.
[Mrs Shirley Wilson]

It was here that he joined the famous 41 Squadron flying Hawker Demons. The following year the squadron returned to the UK, where they converted to Fury IIs and a little later to Spitfires.

In November 1938 came his first promotion from sergeant to flight sergeant. He would have to wait another 17 months before his next promotion but then in April 1940 he was commissioned.

His first major combat occurred at 7.25am on the 28th July 1940, when he shot down a Me109 over the Channel between Calais and Dover. He had seen the plane shoot down his friend Tony Lovell, and could think of nothing but revenge. (The leader of this Gruppe of Me109's was none other than Major Molders of JG51, who belly-landed near the French coast, wounded.) He chased the Me109 out to sea and shot it down.

The following day he was again in action over Dover when he shot down another Me109. However this time his aircraft was hit and he crash-landed his damaged Spitfire (no. N3264) at Manston. Although he was engaged in combat, his next success didn't occur until 15th August, when he shot down a Me110 and damaged another. On this occasion he was slightly wounded in the heel. This did not keep him down, and he achieved considerable success during September, taking care of around 17 enemy aircraft, either shot down or damaged – a remarkable achievement. His final combat on the 28th of this month resulted in his destroying a Me109 over the Channel about four miles south of Brighton.

On the 1st October he was rewarded with the DFC, but what should have been a day for rejoicing turned out to be a day of disaster for him. He was involved in combat with a Me109 over Henfield at 2.55pm and was shot down seriously wounded in the face and head with canon fire. As a result he lost his left eye. He parachuted out and landed at Dunstall's Farm while the aircraft crashed near Albourne. He was quickly taken to Horsham hospital and later moved to Queen Victoria hospital at East Grinstead where the famous Sir Archibald McIndoe worked his magic. So Bennions

Remains of a Me 109 shot down at Falmer, near Brighton, by Ben Bennions on 1st October 1940. [Bill Summers]

Part of Ben Bennions' log book from 1940, recording enemy planes shot down.

became one of the famous 'guinea pigs.' All the patients there were known simply as 'pigs' the hospital being the 'sty.'

Unable to see out of one eye, spattered with pieces of shrapnel and suffering burns he was, he recalled, feeling pretty sorry for himself.

'At the far end of the ward I saw a badly burned airman in a wheelchair. I'd never seen anyone like that before. He came towards me, propelling his wheelchair and, as he got closer I saw that his hands were badly burned and his feet as well. And his ears and his nose. His whole face. It was terrible, really. But, halfway down the ward he picked up a chair with his teeth – I mean, his lips were badly burned but he caught hold of the back of the chair with his teeth – and he rested the two back legs on the platform on the front of his wheelchair and he came on towards me, the new boy, at the entrance to the ward. He stopped beside me, slung the chair off alongside and he said, "have a seat, old boy".

'And I thought, "What have I got to complain about?" And from then on, I started to recover.'

He described McIndoe as a god – a man who, he said, taught him that it was better to live for your country than to die for it.

Between his first combat in July 1940 and his serious wounding he had many other near misses during the Battle of Britain. About 4.15 pm on Saturday 7th September he was landing at Rochford after being involved in combat when his undercarriage collapsed. On this occasion he was unhurt and the Spitfire was able to be repaired. Then came the combat over Maidstone at 4.40pm on Wednesday September 11th, when he suffered his heel wound. A week later saw him in combat once again over Gravesend. His aircraft was damaged, but he was unhurt. On Friday 20th September his Spitfire was damaged in combat and he was forced to land at Lympne at 5pm.

On Saturday 28th September 41 Squadron had been badly mauled by enemy fighters during the morning. About 1.45 pm the same day Bennions was back in the skies again and engaged in a fierce combat with Me109s over Hornchurch. He was flying Spitfire no. R6619 when the fuselage of his aircraft was hit and badly damaged by 20mm canon fire. He was forced to return to base, luckily unhurt apart from his pride. His aircraft was repaired.

He made a very good recovery from the Queen Victoria Hospital but earned himself the nickname of Cyclops – not very flattering , but he saw it as a great joke. He was soon up flying again, but only during daylight hours.

The years quickly passed by and in 1943 he was posted to North Africa as a liason officer with a USA fighter group, but in October he was wounded again by shrapnel when a landing craft in which he was going ashore at Ajaccio in Corsica was sunk.

He left the RAF in 1946 and trained as a teacher. His early days as an aircraft apprentice provided the ideal basis for him to specialise in technical drawing, metalwork and woodwork. He became head of department at Hipswell County School (now Risedale School) in Catterick before he retired after 28 years. He gave up, he said, 'when it became no longer fashionable to enforce discipline in the educational system.'

There was a lot more to George Herman Bennions than many

people knew. For example, he was a skilled worker in silver, even having his own hallmark. He was a pretty good golfer, too, being elected captain of his local club in Catterick before being made an honorary life member. With a few colleagues he built a dinghy and sailed regularly, and for many years he part-owned a Tiger Moth, which he continued to fly well into his seventies.

A row of houses built at the nearby RAF base at Catterick was named in his honour. He married Avis Brown in March 1935 and they had three daughters and a son, who died in infancy. His wife died in 2000 and George himself passed away on 30th January 2004.

The funeral at Catterick of George 'Ben' Bennions, who described himself as 'proud to have lived, rather than to have died, for his country; proud to have been a guinea pig; proud to have met life face to face. Proud – and very thankful.' During the war he was responsible for destroying or damaging 22 enemy aircraft. [Mrs Shirley Wilson]

The 1940 Barcombe Bomber

During the afternoon of Monday 9th September 1940, a large number of German bombers with an escort of Me109s made their way across the Channel for an attack on London. The bombers included Dorniers Do 17s, Heinkel He111s and Junkers Ju88s.

There had been several unsuccessful sorties against London, the Thames estuary and aircraft factories in the morning. The plotters noticed quite large formations massing over Calais-Boulogne, some including more than 30 or 50 planes. In all the enemy aircraft totalled in excess of a hundred, but some formations appeared not to have fighter escorts. A high flying screen tried to draw off the British fighters just before the raids developed.

This time 11 Group were not going to be caught napping. At 5pm, when the raiders began to come in, the British squadrons were in position and waiting. With 11 Group Squadrons to the south of London, and 10 and 12 Group guarding positions to the north of the capital, the stage was set.

It was the German intention to attack targets in London, the Thames estuary and Brooklands, but the fighter interceptions were so successful that they broke up most of the enemy formations before they got to their targets. The German aircraft sent out a number of distress signals, and radio control stations on the French coast ordered formation leaders to break off attacks if either the defences were too strong or that fighter protection was too weak. These messages were heard with great interest, and a wry smile, by British radio monitors in Kent.

Many of the German bomber crews became panicky and jettisoned their bombs over a wide area, including Canterbury, Kingston, Epsom and Purley. However, a few of the bombers did get through and dropped their loads on Wandsworth, Lambeth and Chelsea.

After the enemy had returned to France, the RAF counted 28 German aircraft destroyed, for the loss of 19 British fighters, from which six pilots were recovered. London had been saved from a serious bombing raid.

One of the bombers involved was a Junkers Ju88A-1, no. 5074, which took off from its base in Belgium, and was piloted by Hans Gert Gollnisch.The other members of the crew were Uffz. Willy Rolf, the observer, Uffz. Willi Hamerla, the radio operator, and Uffz. Ernst Deibler, the flight mechanic/rear gunner.

At about 5.40 pm on Monday 9th September 1940, this aircraft was one of many shot down over Sussex and Kent. In all probability it was shot down by F/Lt. Gerald Edge of 253 Squadron, who claimed to have destroyed four Junkers 88s at this time. (*See author's note on page 53.*)

Hans-Gert Gollnisch now takes up the story:

'In early September 1940 my unit, II/KG30, was transferred from Denmark to Chievre near Ath in Belgium. The reason was to concentrate bomber groups for bigger raids on England.

'It was the second mission of this kind, when we took off in Chievre to meet about 200 bombers of all kinds in flight-level 5,000 metres above Cap Gris-Nez. Then, after a wide swing eastwards, we headed for London, escorted by German fighters. The order was to bomb docks and ships on the banks of the Thames.

Members of 11/KG30. Uffz. Willy Rolf is third from the left in the back row. Uffz. Willi Hamerla is third from the left in the front row. [John Dibley]

'The target could already be seen, as our plane was suddenly hit by a short burst of fire – out of machine-guns of a British fighter that had evidently approached from below to a short distance, unseen by the escorting fighters and unseen by our rear gunner. Our plane was badly damaged. The stick did not work anymore; the cable of the elevator must have been hit. Both engines were damaged, the right one losing gasoline, the left one oil

"Then Uffz. Rolf reported that the rear gunner, Uffz. Deibler, was lying dead in a pool of blood. A bullet must have pierced the artery of his neck. In the meantime I had given the order to shed the roof of the cockpit for baling out. But then I found out that the trimming wheel, which could replace to some extent the elevator, was still working. Thinking of our dead rear gunner, I decided to stay in the plane and try to reach the Channel, hoping that the engines would run long enough. I wanted to go down on the water, to get into the rubber dinghy that every Junkers 88 had aboard and maybe reach the French coast. I turned south for the shortest way and dropped the bombs unsharpened. I told the crew, and everybody wanted to stay in.

'But in case we would be attacked by more British fighters we had no weapons to defend ourselves, because the rear gunner was dead, and we had lost the other guns when we shed the cockpit roof.

'Therefore I dived into the clouds 3000 metres below, but there the engines didn't want to start again and I could not even let out the flaps because the electrical system did not work anymore. Flying already too low for baling out, I had to try to make a belly-landing. I was lucky to manage it, because most of the meadows and fields around there [Lewes] were covered with all kinds of obstacles.'

The Junkers 88 landed in a field at Banisters Farm, Toulver Lane, Barcombe, near Lewes, at 5.40pm. Deibler was dead and the other three members of the crew were captured and taken to Lewes police station by Superintendent Holloway, arriving at 7pm. The following day Flt. Lt. Anthony Boning, an RAF intelligence officer from Maidstone, attended Lewes police station and interviewed the German airmen. Willy Rolf was escorted by the Queen's Own West Surrey regiment to Barnet. Hamerla and Gollnisch continued to be detained at the police station until 1.55pm on Thursday 12th

September, when they were taken under escort to the infantry training barracks in Chichester.

The event was later recalled by Rosamund Borradaile, who was spending the weekend in Barcombe, where her eldest sister was taking a few days' leave from ambulance duty in London.

'During the afternoon,' she said, 'while we were working in the kitchen garden, we suddenly heard the noise of a plane overhead – then the rattle of machine guns, followed by a crash. We then realised that a German plane had been brought down in a nearby field: it was a Junkers 88 bomber which had come down in the field next to the orchard of Court House.

'We hurried out to see what was up and saw our gardener, Mr. Fred Tomsett, who was in the Home Guard, approaching from his cottage, carrying a gun, which he told us wasn't loaded! On arrival near the plane we found three occupants standing by and looking stunned, one of them having been wounded in the ear. We asked then how many there were, and the officer in command said "four".

'Later we heard that one of them had been killed, having jumped from the plane. He was a young Austrian airman, Ernst Deibler, whose body was buried in Barcombe churchyard and after the war exhumed and reburied in the German War Cemetery in England [Cannock Chase].

'My sister Violet then went to fetch water from the house, but when she returned she found that the Army had arrived to take the men prisoner and she was not allowed to give it to them (much to her chagrin) – the speed with which they arrived on the scene was exemplary.'

Author's note: I have checked many records of action by pilots involved in this raid, and although two other pilots have claimed attacking Junkers 88s I truly believe that it was acting Sqn. Ldr. Gerald Richmond Edge, aged 26 years, who was responsible. The other pilots involved, and who made claims, were Flt. Lt. Jefferson Wedgewood, aged 23 years, also of 253 Squadron, and FO Gordon Leonard Sinclair, aged 24 years, of 310 Squadron.

'Catseyes' Cunningham's Story

John Cunningham was born on 27th July 1917 in South Croydon, Surrey, the son of an executive at the Dunlop Tyre Company. He was educated at Whitgift School and in 1935 worked on light aircraft at the De Haviland Technical School, which was staffed mainly by students from the school. In November of that year he joined 604 Squadron, Auxilliary Air Force, and in 1938 he became no.4 test pilot for De Haviland – a remarkable achievement for one so young.

No. 604 Squadron was mobilised for war in August 1939 and in May 1940 he was detached to Northolt to test the air dropping of bombs. As a result he missed the unit's day over Holland. The squadron then started

John 'Catseyes' Cunningham.

night fighter operations in Beaufighters, which arrived towards the end of 1940.

His first success came on the night of 19/20th November with Aircraftsman Phillipson, when he destroyed a Junkers Ju88A-5 of 3/KG54 over N. Bridge Norton. Around a month later, while flying over the English Channel he destroyed a Heinkel He111 near the Channel Isles. Another Heinkel, was claimed as a 'probable' over Lyme Regis in early January, and soon after this young Phillipson attained the rank of sergeant. (later still he was promoted to warrant officer)

He was replaced in the spring of 1941 by Sergeant 'Jimmy' Rawnsley, who had been Cunningham's gunner when the unit were equipped with Hawker Demons. They went on to be a formidable night-fighting team. Their first success together came over Gatwick during the night of 12/13th January, when they chased and damaged a Heinkel He111. As the year elapsed, more and more successes came, including three Heinkels in one night, 15/16th April.

By the end of September 1941, they were the undisputed night fighting Aces, as they had either destroyed or damaged more than 22 enemy bombers, no doubt saving the lives of hundreds of civilians in towns and cities up and down the country. He was given the nickname 'Catseyes' – and really hated it!

By the end of the war John Cunningham was credited with a total of 20 destroyed, 3 probables and 7 damaged. It would have been more, but he had various other postings, including visits to the USA.

In 1944 he was group captain – night operations at No.11 Group and he was again called to Hatfield to assess a new aircraft. This was De Haviland's first jet, the Vampire, a wonderful aircraft: 'smooth and fast', was his description.

At the end of 1945, aged 28, he left the RAF and rejoined De Haviland at Hatfield. The rest of his working life revolved around the factory. He was awarded the OBE in 1951 and made a CBE in 1963.

Although he was very well known as a wartime fighter pilot, his name would be wider known for test-flying the De Haviland Comet. The aircraft was conceived in 1943 against the background of the American dominance. The work began in earnest as soon as the war was finished. Geoffrey De Haviland, son of Sir Geoffrey, was the chief test pilot. He was killed in 1946 while flying an experimental Dh108 jet over the Thames estuary. It was then that the job of chief test pilot was offered to John Cunningham. One of his main jobs was to find out why the Dh108 had crashed. This aircraft, with subsequent wing designs, was the forerunner of today's European Airbus.

Soon after Cunningham joined the company the Comet was taking shape. He loved his job of being a test pilot and in 1947 he flew the Vampire to a world record height of 59,460ft without wearing a pressure suit – quite incredible.

The 27th July was not only Cunningham's birthday but Sir Geoffrey De Haviland's birthday too. On this day in 1949 Cunningham flew the Comet to a height of 10,000 feet over Hertfordshire. It was great day for the company, but within two years a series of catastrophic crashes grounded the sleek aircraft. By the time the problems had been sorted out, the Comet had lost its lead in the aviation field to new American jet air liners. It entered passenger service a little late in 1952, but was nevertheless the forerunner of passenger jets as we know them today. I am sure the Comet and John Cunningham will be long remembered by those, like me, who enjoyed many holidays as a passenger in the famous Comet airliner.

He died on the 21st July 2002, just six days before his 85th birthday, and another legend was parted from us.

The Downing of 'Mac' MacKenzie

This is the story of a very skilful Hurricane pilot who, in his own words, made one vital mistake – leading to his being shot down in September 1941 and spending a part of his life as a prisoner of war. Most of his POW life was spent in what is probably the most famous of all camps, Stalag Luft III, made famous by 'The Great Escape.'

I have to admit that I knew little about Ken 'Mac' MacKenzie until I read his enthralling book, *Hurricane Combat*, published in 1987. Once I had, I was determined to make contact with this man and find out more about him.

Wg.-Cmdr. Ken 'Mac' Mackenzie. [K. Mackenzie]

Mac MacKenzie suffered a stroke last year ,and fittingly vowed to tackle the problem as he spent his wartime life – battling against the odds. He has passed his 87th birthday, but his mind belies his age. Like all those Battle of Britain pilots I have come to meet over the past few years, he is nothing short of a hero to me.

This story just covers the few days leading up to his landing on French soil and being captured, but there is much more to him than I am able to relate here.

It was a Friday 13th: unlucky for some, maybe. Briefed to attack Lannion airfield in Brittany, he lifted off at dusk from Britain's most southerly airfield, Predannack. It was 18.50 hours, and as the four Hurricane Mk. IIcs turned to cross the Channel, the feelings of the pilots were not good. They had been briefed to follow a strike on the airfield by Whirlwind fighters of 263 Squadron, but they wondered what good targets there were at Lannion. The four aircraft dipped down to about 200 feet above the waves in order to cross the Channel beneath the German radar.

'We spread out into two flights of two aircraft,' Mac told me, 'on a course of 152 degrees, throttling back to a cruising speed of 230 knots with Red 1 and myself (Blue 1) slightly ahead of our No.2's.

'The weather was hazy with some high stratus cloud, and the sea looked dark and, as usual, cold and uninviting, but calm. Keeping radio silence, we skimmed over the water, settling ourselves into our seats.'

The four pilots were: Red 1 Flt.Lt. Denis Smallwood; Red 2 PO Hordern; Blue 1 Flt. Lt. Mac MacKenzie; and Blue 2 Sgt. Derrick Deuntzer. The four aircraft looked like black crows, painted in their all-black matt finish with just the slight glimmer showing from the exhaust stubs in the now fading light and haze.

The flight had lasted just under 25 minutes as the French coast came into sight. They passed Les Triege islands and the pilots then checked all their instruments, switched on the gyro gun-sights to fire and prepared to attack their given targets.

'Flying in line abreast and 200 yards apart, we dived to attack at 100 feet. Red 1 and 2 attacked the western perimeter and, with my No.2, attacked the east side. As we dived to attack, the flak defences opened up with intense and accurate fire from all sides of the airfield and outside of it. The visibility was poor, even with our canopies open, in the hazy and fading light. The tracer bullets of the flak showed up like fireworks, only more deadly.

'Red 1 and 2 fired long bursts into what looked like dispersal pens without any visible result. With my No. 2 we weaved and fired at buildings and dispersals. I silenced a gun post about a half-mile from the north of the aerodrome. The flak was a constant stream by now and getting more accurate, missing me just by a few feet only as I jinked and could only get in short bursts of fire at the guns. Red 1 and 2 – also Blue 2 – had pulled away, but I was determined to have a last quick attack on my own out towards the coast.

'By now the sky was alive with flak and I was sweating like a pig and very angry with the whole mission. I silenced one more gun position but was then coned by the rest as I passed to the south of the airfield and flying a mere 50 feet from the ground in an effort to upset their aiming.

'Then it happened. I felt the thud, thud of bullets hitting my aircraft in front of me. They hit the engine and radiator, and oil spread across my windscreen. I then felt a sharp crack to my head. I made my way from the airfield gaining height and reached about 1800 feet. The engine sounded very rough and then I got the smell of hot metal, warning me of fire, a pilot's greatest fear. It was now that I realised that I was going to have to bale out.'

He searched for a suitable spot and eventually had to bale out into the sea, probably his best option.

'As I glided down I hastily jettisoned the hood, tightened my harness, peering ahead for the sea, now about five miles from the French coast. Checking the oxygen full on, I selected full flap and switched the landing lights on to judge better my height as we settled towards the sea. About six feet up I stalled the aircraft onto the water at about 70 knots. She struck immediately, slowed rapidly and pitched forward violently, water and spray everywhere, with loud banging and hissing from the rapidly cooling over-heated engine.

'It was an uncanny silence as I undid my harness, broken only by the cracking and hissing steam from the engine. I took off my helmet and eased myself up from the cockpit, as she seemed to be nosing under quickly. This was my last recollection of my actions until I came to some time afterwards floating around in my 'K' type dinghy. I was wet through and sitting in about three inches of water, cold as ice, dazed but alive and in one piece, except for my sore and bloody head.'

The dinghy was very small, and he found himself very much alone in a dark, dismal and wet environment. In his predicament he wondered where it had all gone wrong. He went over his actions, trying to think whether or not it was his fault or just bad luck. At about 11pm he made out the dark shape of the French coast in the distance. He could see a few dim lights flickering, but he had no idea exactly where he was. He guessed that he must be somewhere near Lannion Bay. He had two small paddles and so started to stroke away from the flickering lights, trying to get as far away from the French coast as possible under the cover of darkness.

As he continued to paddle he looked over the day with ever increasing anger. First, the rather hurried briefing for this intruder operation. From recent information there were no enemy aircraft based at Lannion, so why attack it?

He had queried the whole operation and had taken off not in the best frame of mind, determined to give Lannion 'a good going over', and now he had reaped his reward. He continued to paddle but it was hard work and he didn't seem to be getting very far. His head was clearing now and he remembered that there were many fishing boats moored a little way from the French coast. The thought came to him that he might be able to get back to England if he could obtain one of these boats. He turned the dinghy around and headed back the way he had come. It was now about 1 or 2 o'clock and he could see the outlines of some fishing boats. Soon alongside, he selected one about 18 feet in length with a mast and sail. He got on board, tied the dinghy behind and was soon on his way.

Progress was slow, and soon he saw an island. As dawn would soon be upon him, he decided to make for it.

'I moored the boat to some rocks in a cove. It was a craggy island, and I took the dinghy ashore to use for shelter, it being very cold. Tucking it between a sort of low wall and a bush, I got into it and then must have fallen asleep. I next woke, or was awakened, prodded by the rifle of a Kriegsmarine, one of several who stood around me with guns at the ready. Seeing that I was a bit groggy, more from cold and stiffness than anything else I think, one of them helped me up. They took the dinghy and escorted me across the island to the tower, which in fact was the lighthouse and just above a small harbour.'

Now a POW, he spent time in several camps but ended up behind the wire at Stalag Luft III. He wasn't, however, one to sit still and do nothing, and he became actively engaged in all aspects of prison escapes. He helped to build the famous 'wooden horse' – yet another incident to be made into a well-known film.

Mac MacKenzie was awarded the DFC on 25th October 1940 and the AFC on 1st January 1953. He currently lives close to the M1 just south of Leicester. His book *Hurricane Combat* (ISBN 0-903243-08-3) is published by Grenville Publishing.

Bob Doe's Story

This is a story I particularly enjoyed researching and writing. I have been extremely fortunate not only to be in touch with Bob Doe but to have spent several hours in his company at his gorgeous house in Sussex.

Bob paid a high price during the Battle of Britain by having his face smashed to pieces. He had to undergo many operations, but the skill of the surgeons is evident in the fact that it is very difficult to see where these terrible injuries were.

Bob himself will identify them during conversations about those wartime days. The man is a delight to be with, his mind sharp as a button.

A photograph of the then Sqd. Ldr. Bob Doe taken on Ramree Island, Burma, in April 1944.

One thing that comes over very clearly is that he doesn't suffer fools gladly. So what of this man whom I have vaguely described: what makes him tick?

Robert Francis Thomas Doe was born on 10th March 1920 in Reigate, Surrey. His father was a gardener on a small estate and he lived in a house within the estate. His grandmother, who was always dressed in black, lived with the family. He had an elementary school education. In 1925 the family moved to Walton-on-the-Hill, where his father had became the head gardener of a large estate.

In January 1935, aged just 14, Bob took his first job, working in a share transfer office of the *News of the World*. His wages at this time were £4 10s – which he regarded a princely sum in those days.

In the late 1930s, amid growing unease, he joined the RAF Volunteer Reserve and was among the first 600 to be selected for pilot training. He attended evening classes in London, and the flying training was carried out at a grass airfield at Hanworth. His first trip, called 'air experience', occurred on 4th June 1938, Bob now being 18 years old.

Later, he went solo on Ansons, which he says were easy to fly. During this time he was also trained how to act as an officer, with the 'mess' activities being central to it. He clearly remembers listening to the radio broadcast by prime minister Neville Chamberlain on the third of September 1939, declaring that Britain was at war with Germany. A couple of months later he found himself at Leconfield, and a member of 234 Squadron, with no idea what aircraft they were to be equipped with.

It turned out that the squadron had two Miles Magister trainers, and then in mid December a lonely Blenheim was delivered – a good way to fight a war against the might of the German Luftwaffe. A couple of days after Christmas the pilots piled into the Blenheim and flew down to Aston Down and picked up eight more. In March 1940 the squadron were at last equipped with something decent to fight with – Spitfires – and Bob was overjoyed.

The squadron was moved to Church Fenton in May and to Middle Wallop in August. On Thursday 15th August Bob opened his account, taking a half share in the destruction of a Me 110.

'I was flying no. 2 to the CO. When he turned after an Me 110, I followed him, and after he'd shot at it I closed in and fired a good burst which produced startling results. The enemy aircraft turned over and dived down into the sea. This was only the second time I had fired my guns, the first having been into the sea. As I watched my Me110 dive into the sea I felt the satisfaction that I was alive and had not made a fool of myself. At that moment, another Me 110 overshot me from behind. I hadn't seen a thing, but I closed on him and fired another burst that had the effect of just the same thing – the Me110 ploughed straight into the sea. I had shot down two without really knowing what I was doing or, more importantly, knowing what was really going on in the skies around me.'

The following day he shot down two more enemy aircraft, a Me109E and possibly a Dornier Do 18, although the latter may have been a Do 24. On the 18th two more enemy aircraft fell to his guns. A half share of a Junkers 88 on the 21st and another Me109 on the 26th completed a memorable month for the young fighter pilot. He then had to wait until the 4th September before he managed to shoot down his next enemy aircraft. This he did in style by destroying three of them in quick succession.

'On the 4th September we were told to patrol Tangmere and saw a gaggle of 110s going towards Brighton, apparently without any 109 escorts. They formed a circle, a new defensive tactic. It was a large circle, and I dived across the circle and had a shot at two or three as they went past. I succeeded in getting two aircraft to pull out, which were dispatched quite easily. I was on my way home from this massacre, cruising quietly along the south coast, enjoying the view. I dispatched another enemy aircraft, which cart-wheeled into the sea off Littlehampton. I believe that our squadron achieved its highest score on this day.'

This enemy aircraft was almost certainly a Me 110 D/O (no.3390) reportedly shot down in the Channel off Littlehampton during combat with RAF fighters. Hptmn. Von Boltenstern and Fw. Schneider of Erprobungs Gruppe 210 were both killed. The aircraft was lost. This is the only aircraft reportedly shot down in or near Littlehampton on this day.

On the 5th he dispatched another enemy aircraft, a Me109, and another hectic day ensued for him on the 6th: one fighter destroyed, and three Dornier Do 17s damaged. The tally continued on the 7th. After he was scrambled, he climbed for a decent altitude to give himself a better chance against the incoming enemy aircraft.

'On this occasion, I drifted across the path of the bombers, watching the fighter formations until they all seemed to move to one side, after some tasty morsel I've no doubt. When they'd moved away, I dived on the rear Heinkel and saw that I'd hit him, as

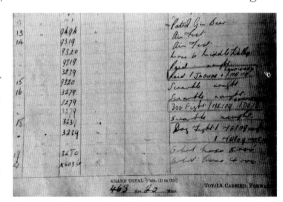

Part of Wg.-Cmdr Bob Doe's log book, recording the destruction of two enemy aircraft on 16th August 1940. [Bob Doe]

he started to lag behind. I pulled up the other side and returned to finish him off before the fighters could get back into position.'

Towards the end of September he was posted to 238 Squadron at Chilbolton, where he changed from Spitfires to Hurricane 1s. His first kill with the new squadron occurred on 30th September when he dispatched a Heinkel He111 over the Channel about 20 miles south of Portland. He had two more successes, when on 1st October he destroyed a Me109 fighter and on the 7th another German bomber, a Junkers Ju88, this time north of Portland.

'On the 7th of October, we were scrambled against what must have been the last daylight bomber raid of the Battle. The bombers were going towards Bristol and we met them just west of Salisbury Plain. I got into the middle of the bombers and managed to damage one, for which I was thankful, as I seemed to be getting quite a lot of hits from somewhere. I then attacked him again, from the rear quarter, and as I was firing saw his tail break off from what seemed to be an explosion just in front of the fin. I found out later that their oxygen bottles were stored there, which could have been the cause. The '88' turned over and spiralled downwards with parachutes coming from the hole at the back. The last man out of the plane pulled his ripcord too early, and I saw a parachute slowly burning as he went down. On returning to base we found 11 bullet-holes in my plane, including one in the engine. From that I concluded that I must have been somewhere near the enemy.'

At this time I am sure he would agree that he had had his fair share of luck, but it was about to run out. On Thursday 10th October, he took off from his base at Chilbolton and, flying Hurricane no. P3984, was soon engaged with enemy fighters over Warmwell.

'On the 10th, four of us were scrambled against a high-flying fighter raid. In retrospect, I don't think Hurricanes should have been used for this purpose. However, we took off and entered cloud at about 5,000 feet, remaining in it all the way up to the raid. By then the other three had disappeared, although I didn't know where.

'My first indication was of a tiny speck of light, which seemed to come over my right shoulder into the instrument panel. A loud explosion under my bottom, a knock on my left hand and a thump as from a hammer on the left hand side of my body. I assumed that the blow on my left chest area was 'it!' – and the one thought I recall with regret was that I would not be able to get married on the 7th of December as had been planned.

'Just after this, I realised that I was still alive and obviously had to do something about getting out of the plane. I pulled the pin which holds the Sutton harness together, but due to the negative 'G' which I was still under, the straps would not release. So, in sheer panic I tried to tear the harness, which must have pulled the straps free and I was then catapulted into space. I then, quite calmly, as I recall, looked for the parachute handle and pulled it. There was an almighty jolt and I was floating downwards at a more leisurely pace.

'I then took stock of myself and found that I couldn't move my right foot or my left arm; blood was everywhere.

'The last part of my descent went far too quickly and I was unable to prepare myself for the landing. As a result, I landed on my bottom and passed out. I had landed on Brownsea Island in Poole Harbour.

'I got married on the seventh of December 1940 as planned, was awarded a Bar to my DFC for shooting down 14 aircraft and returned to flying on the 21st December.'

And so the momentous year of 1940 came to an end.

Having experienced a lovely warm and sunny summer in 1940, the winter of 1940/41 was possibly one of the coldest ever, and Bob would feel this at first hand a few days after Christmas. The Luftwaffe reduced daylight raids but increased night bombing attacks. Since we were not really equipped for night intervention, day pilots were asked to volunteer for night interceptions.

Bob did this on the night of 3rd January. A flight comander, he was taking the CO's place and required a volunteer to go with him. Without hesitation the other flight commander, Jacky Irwin-Mann, volunteered for the task, and they both took off from Chilbolton in perfect conditions. As soon as they were airborne they were ordered to separate at Middle Wallop. Bob was instructed to climb to 15,000 feet on a southerly vector. By the time he reached this height he had crossed the coast and was out to sea.

About ten minutes later he noticed an odd reading on his instrument panel. The radiator temperature was normal, but the oil pressure was rising – although the actual pressure remained good.

He couldn't understand what was going on, so he opened the radiator to cool things down. He reported back to Middle Wallop and they vectored him on a course for Warmwell, that being the nearest airfield. He had no intention of baling out, as the temperature was more than a few degrees below freezing.

Bob Doe today.

He was informed that rockets would be fired through the clouds to give him a location. He slowly lost altitude until he reached around 5,000 feet and then lost contact with Middle Wallop. He was now on his own, in the dark, unable to trust his instruments and with no real knowledge of his location. It was about this time too that the engine packed up in a cloud of sparks, which shot past the cockpit, giving him a further fright.

He finally broke through the clouds and, to his delight, found that he was over the airfield. The moonlight and snow on the ground gave him an idea of the outline of Warmwell. He was aware that the airfield was pear-shaped, with the hangers at one end. He decided that it was wiser to land over the hangers and run into the nearby wood in preference to coming in the other way round.

He made a wonderful approach, keeping his speed up to 160 miles per hour, and with the hangers on his left he went for it. He crashed into a heap of oil drums and was knocked out. The Sutton harness had broken and he had been thrown with some force into the gun sight, breaking his arm at the same time.

'I remember looking up at the sky and it slowly went black as I looked. I put my good hand up to see the reason for this and found my nose in the middle of my forehead!

'The next thing was the arrival of help. I was then carried some distance to what I assumed was the station sick quarters, which in those days had a nursing sister on the staff. This wonderful, motherly voice had her hand in mine; let me pass out at last. I am told it took them half an hour to get the hand free . . .

'I was taken to the local cottage hospital where by great good fortune a local army surgeon was on call. He stitched all the bits back down where he thought they ought to be, and put me to bed.

'I came to sometime the next morning, with a young trainee nurse by the side of the bed. She talked to me and said that Lawrence of Arabia had died in his bed.

'Shortly after that the surgeon arrived and told me that one of my eyes had been knocked out and that he had put it back – he didn't know if it would work. He didn't tell me that my nose had been ripped off and that my upper jaw and the right side of my face had been re-designed.'

He was first moved to an Army hospital in the vicinity, where he remained for the next two weeks, and then to a rather famous hospital called Park Prewett. Sir Harold Gillies had a wing in this hospital, in which he rebuilt people's faces. He was there for a few weeks and underwent several major operations which allowed him

Wg.-Cmdr. Bob Doe DSO, DFC and Bar with his wife Betty. [Bob Doe]

to talk and eat properly again. The men were encouraged to go into the local town, Basingstoke, and even to visit pubs. One of the most popular of these was the Red Lion where there was a big, busty barmaid whom Bob believed to be on the payroll of Sir Harold.

Imagine half a dozen young survivors entering the pub with badly burned and disfigured faces (Bob's, mercifully, wasn't burned) only to find the other customers shying away. Not the busty barmaid, however: she would greet them by saying, 'My darling . . . How lovely to see you!' and would then plant a kiss on each of their faces. What a morale booster!

Having been there a few weeks and undergone about 20 operations, Bob was called in to see Sir Harold one evening. From a 'book of noses' he was asked to choose which he would like to be given. This would entail taking a piece of bone from the inside of his hip, dovetailing it onto his forehead, and then stitching over it what skin there was left.

Bob endured this operation, but two days later he walked into a door and dislodged the bone graft: his nose was, once more, not in the centre of his face.

The effect of the crash, his previous wounds and all the operations left him a rather bad-tempered man. His wife, only 19 years old, found it hard to understand and difficult to cope with.

However, Bob Doe is a very hard man to keep down, and on 15th May 1941 he rejoined the ranks as the 'B' flight commander of 66 Squadron. Three days later he was at Buckingham Palace accompanied by his mother and his wife for the investiture of his DFC and Bar. He had been one of the few Battle of Britain pilots to fly both the Spitfire and Hurricane in combat and was one of the top scorers during this period, with 14 and 2 shared victories

In April 1966 he opted for premature retirement, leaving as a wing commander. He started up his own successful business and enjoys his retirement in Sussex. He was persuaded to write a book about his life and wartime experiences

Eric Barwell's Escape

D uring the course of our correspon- dence, Eric sent me a few pages photocopied from a typewritten manuscript, which included the story of having to ditch his badly damaged aircraft in the English Channel and be rescued by a warship during the Dunkirk evacuation in May 1940. This is a little known story but just the sort of incident I was looking for, and I am indebted to him for his expertise in writing such a wonderful piece. However, the story starts a little before this incident.

It was February 1940, a pretty cold one at that, and Eric was attending a party in

Eric Barwell.

the mess. He had been at RAF Martlesham for only 10 days. The group in attendance were scattered with a few WAAF personnel, and one in particular caught his eye – Ruth Birchall, who was a cypher officer. They were obviously made for each other, later married and lived happily ever after. The subsequent months are detailed in Eric's story but once again space is the enemy.

One day stands out in Eric's memory. On 31st May 1940 the squadron were based at Duxford, flying Defiants, and Eric was waiting to fly to Manston. He took off, and was brought to readiness when the aircraft had been refuelled.

'Round about lunchtime,' he recalls, 'we were ordered up to patrol over Dunkirk docks, where we found much activity both on the beach and in the air. Aircraft, friendly and hostile, seemed to be everywhere. I was the leader of Green section; my gunner was PO Jimmy Williams. He saw his no.2 shoot down a Me109, only to be shot down himself almost immediately. Tracer shells came past my port window. I turned violently to starboard. Williams shot at the chasing Me109, which caught fire and fell into the sea. Aircraft were all over the sky, and I saw one Defiant in four pieces falling towards the sea. I saw no parachutes appear and feared that PO Mike Young and his gunner were lost.

'We returned to base and after being refuelled were put at readiness until late in the afternoon, when we were sent once again over Dunkirk. This time there were more enemy bombers as well as hordes of fighters seriously trying to bomb the men and boats by the beaches. I had one or two inconclusive spars with fighters and then spotted a V formation of Heinkel He111 bombers and a solitary one, which we attacked. Williams gave a long burst of 100 rounds which could be seen entering the under part of the cabin, after which the Heinkel dived rather slowly towards the sea and at about 1,000 feet two parachutes, appeared and the plane crashed into the sea.

'We then attacked the formation of three, which we had seen earlier. Attacking from below, we saw rounds going into the fuselage but with no apparent effect, apart from return fire from the bottom gunner, then whoosh, the cockpit filled with steam and I concluded that a bullet had hit our coolant system somewhere. I throttled back and just then another three Heinkel He111s were seen, at which Williams gave a 30-round burst. I aimed for the Kent coast, having jettisoned the cockpit canopy. I tried to maintain the original altitude of 7,500 feet with minimum revs, but it was unlikely that we could reach the English coast.

'Williams and I had a discussion as to whether we should bale out or ditch the aircraft. Williams said I should decide, and I considered that we should ditch. I was already keeping in sight a thin line of boats and ships stretching between Dunkirk and England and thought we had more chance of being picked up by one of them. Williams said "OK".'

'I had of course been using only enough throttle to maintain a reasonable altitude, but slowly the oil temperature rose until it was off the dial. The engine began to slow down until finally it was going at only a fast tick-over, but at full throttle. I looked to see where to put down. There were motor cruisers, like those on the Norfolk Broads, but of course they were rather small. There were also some fishing boats but I decided against them as they would, I thought, be rather smelly. (I have always wondered since at such irrelevance!) I saw two destroyers steaming towards each other, and about a mile apart. I reasoned that were I to ditch between those, one would have the decency to pick us up.

'The windscreen on the defiant was made of perspex, unlike the conventional fighters that had thick bullet proof glass. Consequently, I undid my Sutton harness and parachute straps, and having told Williams to sit on the fuselage with just his legs in the turret, I stood on the seat and bent down, holding the 'stick' with one hand and the top of the windscreen with the other. The engine had seized up completely and I glided to make a wheels-up landing on the water. Luckily, the sea was smooth, although that made the height difficult to judge.

'I next found myself deep down in the water, although I had previously put a few puffs of air in my Mae West. I swam up and up for what seemed an age before breaking the surface. I then looked around for Williams. He was nowhere to be seen, but I suddenly recognised an object floating: it was the backside of his parasuit. (Defiant gunners wore a special zip-fastening suit enclosing a loosely-packed parachute and a rubber stole inflatable from a Co_2 gas bottle. Williams had accidentally inflated his after the earlier patrol and not replaced the gas bottle.) I swam towards him but could not use the tradional life-saving method of swimming as his parasuit interfered with my legs, so I tried to swim more or less on my side. This was very difficult as his head would keep going under the water. I struggled on and was getting towards my limit to tow Williams when I saw one of the Destroyers slowly coming towards us.

Defiant 1s of 264 Squadron in 1940.

FLYER BIOG

Wing Commander Eric Gordon Barwell was born on 6th August 1913 at Clare, Suffolk and is the younger brother of Group Captain 'Dicky' Barwell, the well-known station commander at Biggin Hill during the early years of the war. He joined the RAFVR in July 1938, training at an airfield near Cambridge, on Tiger moths and Harts, gaining his wings before the war.

He was mobilised on the first day of the war, 3rd September 1939, and for a month he was in charge of a gun post guarding Cambridge airfield. On the completion of his training in February 1940 he was posted to 264 Squadron. In action over Dunkirk and during the Battle of Britain, he survived the Defiant's day debacle. He was awarded the DFC in February 1941 as the unit went over to night fighting, the most difficult form of air combat. In July 1941 he was posted to 125 Squadron as a flight lieutenant, becoming commanding officer in December. In February 1942 the arrival of twin-engined Beaufighters led to the upgrading of this post to wing commander status, and he then reverted to flight commander. He was later 'rested', but returned to 125 Squadron in April 1943. In August 1944 he was posted to FIU, the same month that he was awarded a Bar to his DFC. Here he flew Tempests and Mustang IIIs, but in September he went to main HQ of 2nd TAF as an acting wing , and then to 148 Wing as wing commander flying in April 1945. Late in June 1945 he was posted to command 264 Squadron, until it was disbanded. The circle completed, he was demobilised in September 1945.

During his career he destroyed 9 enemy aircraft including 7 bombers. He also had at least another one damaged and on 10th August 1944 he shot down a V1 (doodlebug).

He left the RAF, returning to his family business in Cambridgeshire, where he remained until his retirement.

'I tried to shout, although it was more like a whisper, I suppose, "Why the bloody hell don't you lower a boat?" Anyway, as I got near the bows of the ship a sailor made a wonderful dive and relieved me of my burden. I went towards the stern where there was a scrambling net, but could not climb it unaided, and then someone tied a rope around me to help me up. As I reached the deck, I was astounded to see Mike Young there to welcome me. (We had given him up as lost during the earlier patrol, but in fact when his aircraft broke up in pieces it took him some time to leave the cockpit, and he did not operate his parachute until down to 2,000 feet. He actually landed in a bomb crater in Dunkirk, unhurt but for a sprained ankle, and caught the first destroyer home.) From the deck of HMS Malcolm, Mike had a grandstand view of my ditching. He said that I apparently stalled the Defiant at about 15ft above the smooth water.

'Williams soon came round. He was lying down and in front of him, framed in a doorway with what appeared to be flames behind him, was Mike Young. Williams immediately thought he had joined Mike in Hell. What looked like flames was in fact the setting sun, but one could understand Williams' wrong conclusion as we had both thought Mike had been killed earlier.

'One of the officers of 'Malcolm' was very kind and lent me a shirt and trousers. I was somewhat stiff, having bruised my knees and left arm. I also had a cut lip, caused by the microphone/oxygen mask I was still wearing when we ditched. (I still have the scar.)

'We docked at Dover, and Mike and I waited for some hours in a naval mess (I believe the Nelson Hotel) before transport arrived to take us to RAF Hawkinge. I carefully hung on to my sodden uniform and flying helmet. We spent rather a short and, for me, a sleepless night and were sent to Duxford the next day. One ear was troubling me, as there was a query as to whether my deep immersion in the water had caused the eardrum to burst. I went to Ely RAF Hospital where it was decided that there was no permanent damage to it, but I was grounded for seven days. On my return to Duxford the CO gave me 48 hours leave.'

FLYER BIOG

Pilot Officer Mike Hugh Young (RAF Service No.42040) was 19 years old at the time of this incident, a young pilot destined to see the war out. He was born in Gloucester on 12th June 1920 and joined the RAF on a short service commission in February 1939.

He completed his training and joined the newly formed 264 Squadron at Sutton Bridge on 6th November 1939. He had a total of 7 destroyed, 6 shared destroyed and 3 damaged. He rose through the ranks and obtained the rank of squadron leader. He was released from the RAF in 1946. He died in January 1998.

A Heinkel at Seaford

This is another story concerning Eric Barwell. At 9.35pm on Thursday 10th April 1941, flying a Defiant Mk.1 of 264 Squadron with Sgt. Martin, he shot down a Heinkel He111H-5, no. 3592, which crash-landed at Blatchington Golf Course, Seaford in Sussex.

The report he submitted on returning to base read: 'I took off with Sergeant Martin as my gunner from Biggin Hill at 20.15 hrs. on 10.4.41 to patrol the Kenley sector. This I did at heights varying between 14–18,000 feet. I was vectored after an enemy aircraft and whilst at about 15,000 feet saw the bandit 500 feet above me and about 1,000 yards ahead, flying on the same course.

'I closed to 300 yards on the beam and slightly underneath and Sergeant Martin opened fire. He got in about four good bursts of one or two seconds each whilst we were closing in from 300 to 50 yards, and we both saw the de Wilde ammunition bursting in the fuselage and engines.

'The enemy aircraft took evasive action by putting his nose up and climbing so that even at 120mph, when the Defiant was almost stalling, we were overshooting.

'As we passed underneath the enemy aircraft, it could clearly be distinguished as a Heinkel He111 and Sergeant Martin had ceased fire as he had been blinded by the flashes of his ammunition. At this moment the enemy aircraft suddenly dived almost vertically into the cloud below and although I followed him I never saw him again.

'As I came out through the cloud, which was about 500 feet thick at 10,000 feet I saw the incendiaries from the enemy aircraft strike the ground somewhere between Redhill and Beachy Head.

'I now understand that the enemy aircraft crashed near the coast and that the crew baled out, which neither I nor my gunner had observed. There was no return fire throughout the combat.

'We claim one Heinkel He111 destroyed. We fired 435 rounds of ammunition and landed back at Tangmere at 22.15 hrs.

'Controlled by G.L. Kenley, which was excellent.

(*Signed*) Barwell.
FO 'B' Flight, 264 Squadron'

The weather during this night was fair at sunset, but with low cloud moving southwards and with mist patches developing through the night. The winds were light and variable.

The Heinkel had a crew of four but also carried a passenger, a reporter. The crew consisted of Lt. Klaus Conrad, aged 23, the pilot; Oberfw. Hermann Platt, aged 25 years, the observer; Uffz. Karl Schwarzer, aged 27 years, wireless operator; and Gefr. Walter Eckardt, aged 20 years, the bomb aimer..The reporter was Karl August Richter, aged 27 years.

The plane took off at 2100hrs from an airfield north-east of Paris, the mission being to attack Birmingham. It carried eight 250kg bombs as well as a number of incendiary bombs. It crossed the English coastline on a NNW course and was flying at a height of 14,000 feet, at a speed of 200kph.

In the area of Redhill, Surrey, it was attacked from below and on the beam by the Defiant, which caught the crew so completely by

Eric Barwell is seen 3rd from the right in the back row of this photograph taken in front of one of the squadron's Defiants.

surprise that they were unable to put up any defence. Both engines were hit during the attack, and with oil pouring out of the port engine, the pilot was forced to switch off the engine. He then jettisoned the bombs and turned back, intending to make for France. The starboard engine overheated and the pilot took the aircraft down through the clouds at a fast rate, levelling out at about 1,000 feet when he gave the order to bale out.

The pilot continued over the sea for a short time in an endeavour to bring his aircraft back to base, but the starboard engine finally caught fire and he returned to landfall, making a crash-landing among anti-invasion wires at Blatchington golf course. The aircraft was well alight by this time, and it burned out on the golf course. The pilot, having proved his

Oberfw Herman Platt, the Heinkel's observer, who was killed when his parachute failed to open. [Susie Ryder]

skill, was then captured with the rest of his crew, apart from Herman Platt. He, too, had baled out, but his parachute failed to open.

RAF authorities interrogated the prisoners at length. The 'AC' lettering on the destroyed Heinkel showed that it came from Stab III/KG 26. The 'gruppenstab' as such had been disbanded, and the personnel and aircraft had been placed in a special staffel, the 10th, which had at least six aircraft.

The crew in general were co-operative and their morale was described as good. However, the exception was the youngest crew member, Gefreiter Walter Eckhardt who, while only 20 years of age, was bombastic, stubborn and confident of the outcome of the war. Later, they were allocated to their POW camps.

Oswald Fischer's Story

O swald Fischer was a young man whose main aim was to be a fighter pilot, fighting for the Fatherland. His wish was granted when he was posted as an unteroffizier (uffz. for short, and the equivalent of an RAF sergeant) to the 3rd.Gruppe of JG 26 -- a highly skilled and professional arm of the Luftwaffe.

Many official records failed to survive the war, but from those that are left it is possible to trace a little of Fischer's progress. The first entry in the records show that he joined the 3rd. Gruppe, with Uffz.Viktor Hager, Uffz. Alfred Niese and Uffz.Erich Schwarz, on 1st. October 1941.

His first combat mission was on 17th. December,1941, when he was assigned to fly the wing of the staffel kapitan Oblt. Mietusch. They intercepted a flight of Spitfires but were caught beneath them. As Mietusch banked, Fischer could not follow and fell out of turn. When he regained control, he was right behind a Spitfire and shot it down – or so he thought (no RAF combats have been traced).

On the 12th. February 1942 the German's launched Operation Donnerkeil, with a very large German convoy moving up the

The Me 109 crash-landed by Uffz. Oswald Fischer at Beachy Head on 20th May 1942. [G. Beard]

Channel, led by the fleet's flagship, Scharnhorst. Gp/Capt Beamish of 91 Squadron, flying over the Channel, reported that 'it was the largest formation of enemy shipping seen in the channel since the Spanish Armada'.

Various gruppes of JG 26 took off during the day to protect the convoy as it moved up the Channel. Fischer, together with Uffz. Georg Pistor, flying Focker Wulf 190s, took off from Coquelles at 12.15pm on their first mission. At 3.46pm they were in the air again in their Fw190s on the gruppe's third mission. On this mission they were forced to keep their distance from the fleet by anti-aircraft fire.

On or about the 10th. March 1942, Fischer was transferred to a new unit, 10(Jabo) JG 26. This transfer was deemed punishment for laughing at his kapitan, Oblt. Mietusch, when he fell off his horse.

On the 20th.May 1942, flying a Me109F-4/R1, together with his partner, he took off on his 31st Jabo mission. They attacked shipping in the Channel, bombing and machine-gunning them, the time then being a little after midday. The ships, while defending themselves, hit Fischer's Me109. He crash-landed on downland at Beachy Head in Sussex. He was unhurt, arrested and spent the remainder of the war as a POW.

Here Oswald Fischer tells the story of that day.

'On the 20th. I was ordered by Hptm. Plunser to lead a mission. I worked out a raid to Brighton, since we had not visited that area for some time, and few wanted to fly there because of the long stretch over the water. I found a Feldwebel who was willing to accompany me as my wingman.

'I planned to go inland about 20 miles before we hit the harbour, and so we did. All worked out fine – low flight over the Channel and hedgehopping over the British countryside and right into the harbour at Brighton. I saw a large ship and told my wingman, "Let's hit it hard!" and in we went. The flak sprayed like a fire hose, but we made it and struck the ship with both bombs.

'As we exited, I got hit. I could hear the impact, but everything seemed to be all right. As soon as we were over the water, my temperature gauge shot up to 'hot' and I could smell the coolant, so I told my wingman to keep going in low flight towards home base. My engine started to smell very bad. I turned around and belly landed my airplane in a field. I tried to blow it up, but the explosive charge would not go off. I became a POW. I regretted my fate, but it was better than drowning in the Channel.'

The diary for 20th. May 1942 records that 'The Jagdstaffel flew fruitless patrols and alarmstarts. The Jabostaffel raided Brighton.' The Jabo pilots were flying several missions a week during this period. Little documentation of these raids has survived other than the casualty reports that were written after each of their frequent losses.

The official time given for Fischer's aircraft being hit by flak from the ship was 12.05pm.

Uffz. Viktor Hager, who joined 3rd Gruppe at the same time as Fischer, was killed in action on 9th October 1942. Flying a Focker Wulf 190A-4, no. 7043, he was shot down at 11.20am by return fire from a B17, which he was attacking in the vicinity of Chemin de Mesnine. He baled out but was unable to open his parachute because of his injuries.

Uffz. Erich Schwarz went on to become a very good pilot, claiming more than 10 allied aircraft shot down or severely damaged.

The Brave Pole

I first read a little of this story in the Brighton *Argus* newspaper a few years ago and was fascinated by what I read. I contacted Stan Jozefiak, and am now pleased to count him and his wife Margaret among my friends. The account is given mostly in his own words, although he has left out the many hardships he had to endure while travelling from Poland to England in order to fight on our side.

Stanislav Jozefiak and his wife Margaret. [S. Jozefiak]

'It was Tuesday 27th May 1941 and after my training I was posted to 304 Squadron at Syerston where they flew Wellington bombers. I was 22 years of age at this time. The day started brightly, hazy sun but warm and pleasant. This gave no hint as to what was in store for me during the next 24 hours.

'During the morning after breakfast and before dinner we took off for around an hour's flight in order to check the aircraft instruments and equipment. We landed, and the ground crew took over in order to fuel up and to load the bombs.

'We were called to attend the briefing for that night's target and the officer informed us that our target was to be Boulogne. That was a short flight for us, and we were happy about that. However we knew that the port was heavily defended with a large number of anti-aircraft guns, searchlights and radar, as well as a number of fighter stations that were quite close to the town. The officer also gave us instructions on how to reach the target avoiding the anti aircraft guns and searchlights. He wished us good luck and a safe return and we then left the briefing room. My crew consisted of Flt. Lt. Bronislaw Kuszczynski, the pilot and captain; PO Jan Woroczewski, second pilot; FO Cezary Wieczorek, navigator; Sgt. Josef Nilski, wireless operator/ air gunner; myself, Sgt. Stanislaw Jozefiak, wireless operator/air gunner; and Sgt. Jozef Drodz, air gunner.

'Soon after teatime we had a few hours of relaxation, although mentally that was always quite difficult. The time soon passed and soon after 10pm we were waiting in the hanger room ready to be taken out to our aircraft for the night's operation. During these operations no one was allowed to leave the airfield for security reasons. We went to our Wellington 1C Bomber, no. R1392 NZ, and took our positions within the aircraft.

About 10 minutes before take off the pilot started the engines so that they would be at the correct temperature, and to check their power and reaction at take-off time. We all checked our equipment and checked in that all was ready. We moved slowly forward to the start point and awaited the green light before taking off. We were third on the line and soon the two Wellingtons in front of us were airborne. We got the green light, and with the full power of the engines we started moving forward, and nearly at the end of the airfield the aircraft slowly lifted up into the air. The time was about 22.45 hours on a warm May evening, not yet dark, and we set course for our target, the French port of Boulogne. From the time we took off we flew in a southerly direction, increasing height all the time. We passed London on the left hand side and could see a few search-lights and guns firing – the Germans must have come over at the same time to bomb London.

'Our target was approaching very fast, and it was easy to make out the French coast. With the searchlights and guns firing, it was most likely that the aircraft in front of us had already been over the target. I was the front gunner and had a perfect view; I was able to direct the pilot to the target until the navigator took over. He gave the instructions to the pilot, saying left or right, and then pushing the button releasing the bombs over the target.

'Immediately after the bombs had gone the anti -aircraft guns scored a direct hit on our aircraft. It went up about 20 feet, and then went out of control down towards earth. I have no idea how long we were going down, but the pilot gave the order to bale out. It was impossible to do anything while the aircraft was going down. It was worse for me, as I needed someone to open the door to release me from the front turret. My situation was desperate and I knew that little short of a miracle could save me. I was pretty frightened and saw my life flash away in front of me.

'The only thing I could do was to pray, and so I prayed to Our Lady of Skalmierzyce, where I was born. I had prayed to her in my younger years, and I prayed for the help I so desperately needed at this time. My prayers were soon answered. The aircraft had dropped several thousands of feet out of control, with the pilot desperately trying to regain some sort of control. He did eventually recover the aircraft, and once he had steadied the plane I was released from the front turret. We were all very badly shaken up and very thankful that the pilot once again was in control. However, it was very dark by now and impossible to access the damage that had been caused to our aircraft.

'What soon became apparent was that one of the engines wasn't working; the port engine had been hit. We soon realised that the rear air gunner, Sgt. Jozef Drodz, was missing. It was probable that he had baled out earlier when the pilot gave the order. He was never found; most likely he drowned in the English Channel.

'With only one engine in full working order as well as other damage, we were being rather hopeful that we would make it back across the Channel to home soil. We were hoping to land at the nearest airfield in the south of England, but just in case we came down in the Channel we removed the Astra Cupola [the glass or perspex dome housing the guns].

'We were gradually getting across the Channel, although we were losing height all the time. Then the other engine suddenly caught fire. The pilot again ordered us to bale out as the aircraft once again dived towards the earth. At this time I was near the Astra Cupola, which had already been removed, with my parachute already attached. I managed to get to where the Cupola had been, but with the aircraft going down, gathering speed as it did, I only managed to get half of my body out. I knew I had to do something, and quick. In desperation I pulled my parachute cord handle, not giving a thought that the tail of the plane might cut me in half. The opening parachute must have missed the tail of the plane, just, but pulled me out of the burning aircraft. I had no idea at this stage what was happening to everyone else. I don't know if anyone else had ever baled out via the Cupola, but under the circumstances I had no choice. It was truly a miracle that I came down alive.

'The aircraft must have been very low when I baled out, as it only took a few seconds before I could see trees in front of me, instead of the sea that I really thought I was landing in. I came down very fast and could not avoid the trees. Suddenly I crashed into a large tree or branch before I finally landed. Hitting the tree was extremely painful but the real pain was in my left leg. I was unable to stand and could make out the shape of a building not too far away. I started to crawl along the ground dragging my left leg behind me. It hurt every time I moved, but I knew I had to get help. I thought about my colleagues and wondered where they might be. Had they landed somewhere near? I called out, but nobody answered. I continued crawling towards the building that I think was a fire engine shed, unmanned during nightime.

'I called for help several times and I eventually saw some lights flickering here and there, but help didn't come straight away. I continued to shout for help; the pain was by now excruciating. The home guard of the district took time to get organised and eventually got the courage to come and see who I was. Six men appeared, armed with hayforks and sticks. They at first thought I was a German parachutist as they expected an invasion at that time. They shone their torches on me and saw that I was wearing my RAF uniform. I explained to them what had happened and soon they were only too pleased to help me.

'I had landed at a small village called Hatfield near to Tunbridge Wells, and very soon I was on my way to the local hospital where the doctors and nurses were waiting for my arrival. They first cut my left flying boot off, then split and removed my trousers. I was then given an injection and asked to count to ten. I have no idea how many I counted, as the next thing I knew was waking up about teatime, in a nice clean bed. My left leg felt as though it was on fire and I still had the terrific pain. I kept asking as to what had happened to my colleagues, and after a few days I found out the terrible news. Jozef Drodz baled out somewhere over the English Channel; his body was never recovered. Josef Nilski also managed to bale out, but he never flew again after this event. The three remaining members of my crew, all officers, were killed when the plane crashed at Darwell Hole, about 11 miles north-west of Hastings.

'They were buried in the Polish Air Force cemetery in Newark, Nottinghamshire.'

Stanislaw Jozefiak is one of those incredible people whose story is stranger than fiction. He is made of the stuff that films are made of ,building up the heroism as the film unfolds – except that he is the genuine thing, a real hero and not a celluloid one made in Hollywood. His story starts on 10th September 1919, when he was born in a small town called Skalmierzyce in the region of Poznan, Poland. He was one of seven children, four girls and three boys. Life was very hard, and when his younger brother was born his father immigrated to France, finding work in a steel factory and sending money home to his family. He worked there for 10 years.

The family were brought up with a strict religious background. From an early age Stanislaw dreamed of being able to fly a plane, and he later joined an air Force cadet school. The three-year course consisted of military training and general education in the first year, followed by technical education and training to specialise as a pilot, radio operator or aircraft mechanic. He was still at the school when war broke out and German forces invaded Poland. Together with many of his compatriots, he decided to come to England, join the RAF, fight the Germans and help free his beloved Poland. He had an extraordinary journey that first took him southwards into Rumania. He managed after a struggle to reach Constanza, and crossed the Black Sea to Turkey. He then reached Greece and travelled by ship via Beirut, Haifa, Alexandra and across the Mediterranean to Marseilles. That in itself was a massive journey, but there remained some distance before he could reach his destination.

The date was now 20th November, and he soon joined up with other Polish airmen in France and began training. He spent Christmas 1939 there before moving up to Le Havre and finally to England, arriving in Southampton.

After the collapse of France, some 5,500 out of a total of 7,600 men in the Polish Air Force escaped to England during June and July 1940, arriving by devious routes. Special Polish fighter squadrons were set up, and they fought with great distinction. By February 1941 there were eight Polish squadrons; this was about an eighth of the total strength of the RAF Fighter Command. Soon there were four bomber squadrons, too. After completing his gunnery course in Scotland Stanislaw was posted to RAF Benson. He received more training at 18 OTU and after another couple of training programmes was posted to RAF Syerston about five miles from Newark-on-Trent, a new airfield opened in December 1940. The first bomber squadrons to be posted there were the 304 and 305 Polish Squadrons.

He completed 53 bombing operations with a total of 398 hours operational flying hours to his credit. He was promoted to warrant officer during his service and decorated with the Virtuti Militari, the highest Polish military cross, and four times with the Cross of Valour (Krzyz Waleczny).

His dream was always to become a pilot, and in 1943 his chance came along. He was posted to RAF Hucknall, near Nottingham, in July 1943 and later to Brighton, staying in one of the seafront hotels. He attended lectures at the Hotel Metropole and enjoyed his visit to Brighton. He returned to Hucknall at the end of 1943 flying solo in Tiger Moths. His flying hours increased, and after many training courses and being based at several different RAF airfields his dream eventually came true. At the beginning of 1945 he was posted to RAF Rednall near Shrewsbury, where he was soon flying Spitfires and Mustangs. He was posted to 317 Polish Spitfire Squadron in Germany as part of the 2nd Tactical Air Force Group. At the end of 1946 the squadron left Germany for the last time, and soon the Spitfires would be scrapped – but not before Stanislaw completed more than 500 operational hours flying a wonderful aircraft. He states that he couldn't help shedding a tear or two when his beloved Spitfire was dumped, knowing that shortly it would be smashed up as scrap metal.

What an end for a super aircraft: criminal, plain criminal!

There is a lot more to Stanislaw's life than these few brief words. More can be found in a book he wrote called *God, Honour and Country*. When the war ended he gave up his uniform and returned to civvy street. After a while he met and married Margaret, and settled down to family life. He was very happy but one thing always bugged him: where did his aircraft crash? He dearly wanted to honour his fallen crew, a desire that grew stronger as each year passed. Then, after close on 60 years, he had a stroke of luck. In 2000 he travelled from his home in Derbyshire to attend a memorial service at Chailey in East Sussex to honour three Polish combat squadrons. Seizing the opportunity, he added one day to his schedule in the hope of finding the place where his bomber had crashed. He asked a lot of questions and was given the name and address of David Martin, who lived between Heathfield and Battle. With his help the exact site was at last located. The plane had crashed into a large old oak tree – and the tree was still there.

Stanislaw Josefiak's memorial to his fallen comrades. [S. Jozefiak]

He returned home with ideas for his personal memorial taking shape in his mind. He finally set about the painstaking task of erecting this tribute to his fallen comrades, travelling down from Derbyshire weekend after weekend The base was soon put in place and from that point the memorial gradually grew – a few inches, a few more inches, a few feet as the plaque grew in height. Occasionally he would stand back to admire his work and, with sadness, to remember his former friends.

Wiping away a tear or two, he continued his work of love. At the end he was working 12-hour days, desperate to complete his work before the anniversary of the crash on 27th May.

Wallace Cunningham's Capture

On the 28th August 1941 Wallace Cunningham, a flight commander with 19 Squadron, took off from his base at Matlask, a satellite station of Coltishall, to escort a number of Blenheim Bombers.

Wallace Cunningham.

The operation was a low level attack on shipping in Rotterdam harbour. This was deemed to be a large raid by British bombers, but a stiff price was paid. The Blenheims came from several squadrons, including 21, 88 and 226, and they suffered heavy losses. A total of seven bombers were lost and several more were damaged. Another crashed on take-off from RAF Wattisham. Five crew members were taken prisoner but 16 were killed on the raid.

This wasn't to be a good day for Wallace either. As it was a low-level attack he was ordered to fly his Spitfire almost at sea level.

"We took off at 4pm after a two hour delay," he later recalled, 'escorting two squadrons of Blenheims, to bomb a target in Rotterdam harbour. We were flying close to sea level and I can still see the tracks made by the twin engines of the bombers. We were ordered to keep down, as the Blenheims wanted the maximum advantage of surprise, although we as escort were no help in not being high enough to attack enemy fighters that might arrive on the scene. However, we might act as a distraction and draw the fire.'

The group were met by the German defences, and one by one the Blenheims were shot down. The Spitfire escorts fared little better.

'I had succeeded well in keeping low crossing the Channel, but as I reached the coast I was shot down by multiple pom-pom canon fire. Our CO, Sqn. Ldr. 'Farmer' Lawson, and Peter Stuart, my no. 2, were also shot down, and both were killed. My Spitfire engine was hit by this shell fire. I knew I had a problem and also that I had to gain height in order to bale out. I tried desperately to climb, but as the glycol was leaking badly the Merlin engine was starting to seize up. I knew that was it. I gave no thought to becoming a POW, just to get down safely. I came down on the sandy beach right in front of a gun post. Looking back now, I was 23 years old, a bit older than many of the lads in my squadron. During the previous few weeks I had started to suffer with getting sties in my eyes, and I had a couple of abscesses lanced by the doctor under anaesthetic. This was a sure sign of tiredness and I should really have taken a rest from flying. Mind, I was about to get my rest, albeit unplanned. I suppose my first thoughts should have been to look around for means of escape, but that was really out of the question, certainly in front of a gun post.

'However, I was congratulating myself on getting down to terra firma safely and uninjured, with undercart up and with no power in the engine. I obviously didn't know then, but I had 46 months of captivity in front of me.

'Just then the machine gun opened up over my head, and I certainly got the message.'

He was taken away, and after a short while found himself in the officers' mess, where he was ushered to sit down on a sofa. He was feeling pretty sorry for himself. His first thoughts were for his family at home; then his squadron colleagues; lastly, the thought of the unknown, what was about to happen to him. A few hours elapsed and he was taken by ambulance to a gaol in Amsterdam, where he spent a couple of days in solitary confinement.

He soon found himself in company with two other RAF Officers being taken up the Rhine to Frankfurt and to Dulag Luft, a Luftwaffe intelligence camp, where he was again put into 'solitary'. Later he was interrogated. The German officer's English was perfect. Wallace was surprised to learn that he knew more about the mission than he himself did, explaining the delay and telling him that the wing commander who was to lead the mission had suffered engine failure on take off and was killed. This was confirmed later by a flight lieutentant from Bomber Command who had also taken part in the raid on Rotterdam. Had there been a leak?

'Having had a chance to relax, the sties and abscesses that had been troubling me started to disappear, thank goodness. I spent a few days in solitary. I think because my interrogator had decided that I was a waste of his time, I was admitted to the general camp compound. This was a small enclosure with 8–10 huts, contained in what I leant was the standard arrangement of a 10ft-high stockade, a double wire fence with rolled razor wire on top. There was also a tripwire about 20 feet inside, giving a piece of 'no-mans land'. There were also machine gun and searchlight posts at regular intervals.

'The main gates were opened and we three newcomers walked in. I was surprised to be welcomed by a member of my flight, Dennis Cowley, not a little annoyed. He had been shot down a week or so before while standing in for a lad, Oxlin. He had been bitten by my dog in a fight with Flash, 'Grumpy' Unwin's alsatian. Needless to say Dennis blamed me for his current predicament.

'Life in Dulag Luft was rather relaxing and we seemed to get enough food to eat, also to catch up on the latest RAF gen. Early in September we moved off *en bloc* by cattle trucks to a camp at Lubeck Oflag XC. This was an army-run camp and full of the bitterness associated with the bombing of Hamburg and district that had become routine. This was borne out by the fact that we didn't get any Red Cross parcels, only a few slices of bread, a few potatoes and a bowl of cabbage soup each day. This wasn't enough to fulfil our needs, and we were hungry for a lot of the time.

'An early aggravating, but probably routine, event was the confiscation of our RAF clothing. In exchange we received tatty old Polish khaki trousers, which were certainly not made to measure; this seemed to merit a sketch. (In my diary.)

'The Germans seemed to have a problem deciding when to switch off the main camp perimeter lights during the frequent air raids. One night an inaccurate bomb-aimer hit the camp. As luck would have it the damage occurred to the German officers' mess. That didn't help us particularly, but we got a lot of pleasure from watching the British Army prisoners who were brought in to handle the demolition and debris clearance. The bricks were passed around one to the other in such a way that the pile never grew less.

'Like many others, I hadn't contemplated life as a POW, and I certainly had a lot to learn. One third of our RAF pay was deducted back home and paid to the Germans through the Red Cross. Our captors paid this to us in the form of lagergeltcamp money, which could not be used for the purchase of anything useful such as food, cigarettes or the like. I remember specifically things such as clothes pegs, erzatz mustard and tomato paste, the latter made from tomato skins, dyestuff and salt. The mustard at £4 a can we threw away, but kept the can in which to wash our smalls. The tomato paste mixed in hot water decreased the pangs of hunger for a minute or two but then caused frequent trips to the loo – a claimed record being 13 times in one night. Using a fat-lamp during black-out while visiting the loo gave rise to a bullet or two being fired along the corridor. Arising

One of the cartoons drawn in his POW diary by Wallace Cunningham.

from these events, these sufferers learnt to keep an empty tin, a Klim tin (milk backwards). This was very convenient, but not so funny for the occupant in the lower bunk with a careless type sleeping above.

'One day towards the end of 1941 we were marched down to the railway station and onto cattle trucks and, with a variety of hold-ups, eventually arrived at Warburg Oflag V1B. We seemed to have been joined on arrival by some other RAF officers, some Ack-Ack and Anzac REME officers, who were taken prisoner during the fall of Crete and Greece. Various other POWs also joined up at this new camp with Maj.Gen. Victor Fortune, a pair of brigadiers, a plethora of colonels, majors etc. and all the officers captured at St. Valery, left behind in France. There were other Army personnel. The total of all of us was some 3,000 Allied prisoners.

'We had to amuse ourselves during the long hours, and so amateur theatricals took up a lot of time. Some of the more well known performers with us at this time included Rupert Davies, who later took the part of Maigret on TV, and David Tomlinson, the well known film and stage actor. Another one who became a public figure was the Australian pilot Joe Beirne, a very competent stage carpenter, who after the war became the prime minister of Tasmania.

'The camp padre was Church of Scotland, who was captured at St.Valery. His services were very well attended and gave us the opportunity of belting out the national anthem as a hymn. This was returned by, we believe, members of the Africa Korps marching around the outside of the wire singing 'Wir marchen gegen England.'

It is well known that POWs were made up of very skilful people. They were determined to harass and annoy their German guards as much as possible without mortal danger to themselves. They became adapt at making articles impossible to believe from bits of rubbish – for example, earphones fashioned from a round cigarette tin, a plastic lid from a pickle jar and razor blades split in half, softened and laminated. These were needed for listening in to a radio set that was also made from odds and ends, and very skilfully engineered.

'Douglas Bader, who was also with us in Schubin, following up his creed of always causing trouble for the Germans, got me involved in digging a short tunnel. Yes, once more, from an abort in our own compound and in normal use. He, of course, wouldn't get very far if he got out, but it would be a great tale for him. The "sales" talk was good: the distance from the edge of the pit nearest to the tripwire was perhaps 20ft, about 20ft to the double barbed wire stockade, in itself about 8ft wide, plus a margin to get clear of the wire outside, a total of about 60 feet. The tunnel was not very far below the surface and we hurried it. The tunnel was not properly controlled by compass in order to measure it to be straight and true. When the time came to abort, 12 POWs were in the tunnel; Douglas and I were in favoured positions and opened up the exit at 1am to find that the distance wasn't correct. We found ourselves directly under one of the perimeter lights. There was only one thing for it, to crawl backwards

A healthy lack of respect: another of Cunningham's pointed cartoons.

in the darkened 2ft-square tunnel to our huts. I can still clearly recall Bader, his tin legs clanking like the tin man in Over the Rainbow, and dragging his rations across the parade ground.

'The German guards did their usual thing to discourage any further digging in that location. They brought in a full 'honey wagon' (that's a wagon full of sewage) and made the Russian prisoners empty it in our knocked in tunnel.'

Wallace was moved to other camps during his captivity, ending up in Stalag Luft III, the camp made famous by The Great Escape.

'Another tunnel on which I helped was that termed the Wooden Horse. It was successful as a tunnel and also as an escape. Good planning and good support in carrying the vaulting horse out and in over a number of months needed faithful assistants. Firstly, the horse had to be built, able to carry on internal racks two diggers and, at the end of the shift, the bags of excavated sand as well. The horse and contents were carried out on a dry day, to its fixed place, as near to the wire as possible, without its looking ridiculous. The inmates got on with the job of opening up and getting to work. Two stout pieces of timber were slid through the horse able to take the weight with four carriers, being careful not to look overloaded. All day, often until late in the day, we jumped over the vaulting horse, often fed-up and wondering when the knock would come. Of course those down below didn't know it was getting dark.'

The wonderful story of the Wooden Horse escape is well known, and the tunnelers made it to safety. However, the most famous example of all was 'the Great Escape,' when 76 POWs got away from the camp. The terrible murder of 50 of them by the Gestapo ensures that this incident will never be forgotten.

'I spent the longest part of my captivity in Stalag Luft III, a large camp at Sagan in Poland for Airmen, mainly RAF officers. It was run by the Luftwaffe and we expected some mutual understanding, and as long as the Gestapo were not involved, this was so. One day, the camp commandant had to announce to us that some 50 escapees were shot 'trying to escape': he also was more than a little ashamed. Our security officer, a very important post, was one of those who was shot and murdered. The winters in Poland were very, very cold, none worse than in the winter of 1942.

'Later on we were quite versed in how the war was going and knew that the British and American forces were coming from the west while the Russians were heading in from the east. The RAF prisoners were evacuated from Stalag Luft III in January 1945, when the sound of the Russian guns could be heard from the east. Guided by the Luftwaffe guards, we wandered erratically, generally westward, in the snow for two to three weeks, ending up in Luckenwalde, behind the Elbe, west of Berlin, a miserable place, infested with French lice.

Then came a day in early May 1945 when the German guards started to reduce in numbers, then totally disappeared. We knew that the Americans were close to us, just the other side of the Elbe river. We also knew the Russians were closer. One day I went out foraging with a Yankee soldier on a motor cycle combination with two jerry cans. I needed some petrol for the generator in the camp – we had no workable pump to work the sewage system. We caught up with a front line Russian band, like gypsy travellers. There was a lieutenant, three Russian soldiers, one female and one German prisoner who was the dogsbody. Without any knowledge of Russian we tried to scrounge some petrol but right away were ordered to repair a puncture in their open bed lorry. The Yank and I weren't too happy about our position, but when the repair was done we got a jerry can full of petrol.

'Within three or four days we had a clear cut take-over by the Russian Army. A tank knocked down the main gate to the camp and they set up to take our particulars. We learnt that we were being returned via Russia, and attempts by the Americans to get trucks over the Elbe to collect us were frustrated. A month after, peace was declared and the Russians delivered us in their trucks to a point on the Elbe where American forces were waiting.

'It was magic to be back in friendly hands.'

Wallace Cunningham sent me a lengthy and very detailed written manuscript about his life behind the wire. It is a superb story, and only space dictates my sadness at having to précis it. I am sure that over the years I shall be able to use certain passages from his work and allow other people the luxury I enjoyed of reading his wonderful and moving story.

He took every opportunity to be involved with prison life – in fact, he went a little further and made a series of pencil drawings which he had copied and sent to me. As with his script about life behind the wire, there is too much to publish here.

He was demobbed on 1st September 1945, was married and lived in Kent until 1960. At this time he had become chief engineer of Winget, a well-known name in the civil engineering and building construction world which sadly is no longer in existence. In 1960 he returned to Glasgow, his birthplace, to a subsidiary of the Hanson Group. He retired in 1981 as director sales and engineering and currently lives in Scotland.

Joe Kayll's Story

Joseph Robert Kayll was born in Sunderland on 12th. April 1914. He entered the family timber business when he left school in 1928, but in his later teens he became more and more interested in aircraft and flying. He joined 607 Squadron, Auxiliary Air Force, and in 1934 he learned to fly. During the early few months of 1939 he became a flight commander and was mobilised with that unit in August of that year.

He was posted to France with the Squadron on 15th November. He was still in France when in March of the following year he was promoted to command the sister squadron, 615. This unit was heavily involved in the Blitzkrieg of May 1940 until its withdrawal back to England towards the end of the month. During the retreat, the unit's travelling office, containing its record books and the pilots' log books, was destroyed by a bomb.

There is very little detail of this period to have survived. By this time Joe Kayll held the rank of squadron leader and had been awarded both a DSO and the DFC, the citations crediting him with nine victories. However, being the modest man he is, he reckons that it was probably seven victories, not nine: the numbers aren't very important, but it proved what a superb fighter pilot Joe Kayll was even at this very early stage of the war.

During this time the unit was re-equipped, but it turned out to be rather a short break as the squadron was operational again during the last week of June. This was just as well, as it was just moving into Britain's most crucial period of the war, the Battle of Britain. Sqn. Ldr. Joe Kayll was to be involved in the very thick of the action.

It was while flying his Hurricane 1, no. P4221, on Friday the 16th August 1940 that he claimed a probable on a Heinkel He111 a few miles south of Brighton when the German bomber was making a run for home. (This was almost certainly the Heinkel of 7/KG55 which force landed near Worthing.) Two days later, on the 'hardest day', Sunday 18th, the airfield at RAF Kenley was targeted by a low level attack by 9 Dornier Do 17s, which flew low over Seaford, following the River Ouse up to Lewes and then along the railway line to

Kenley. This was closely followed by a much larger force flying at a high altitude, consisting of a hundred or more bombers and about 60 escort fighters. He found himself in the midst of a great German aircraft Armada, with the odds pretty poor for the British pilots. At 1.40pm, towards the end of the raid and flying Hurricane no. R4220, he shot down one of the escort Me109s. He continued to be successful in attacking enemy aircraft and in claiming German aircraft destroyed as well as damaged.

By the end of October he had his name against 23 German aircraft, destroyed, probable and damaged, either by himself or shared. This in turn put him in the league of top British fighter Aces.

In December 1940 he was posted to HQ. Fighter Command, as squadron leader tactics. Although it was a useful rest, he hankered to be operational again. He returned to the fray on the 2nd June 1941, after another promotion, to wing commander flying, at Hornchurch.

On 25th July he flew as no.2 to the station commander, Gp/Capt Harry Broadhurst, on a 'nuisance' raid with two other aircraft. Harry Broadhurst took the section back over a target soon after a raid. As they climbed into the sun they were bounced by Messerschmitt 109s of JG 26, and Joe Kayll and the two other pilots were shot down. He managed to crashland in a field near St.Omer.

'I think we were about 20,000ft,' he said later, 'when the 109s jumped us out of the sun. My engine continued to run, but with no power. I had the idea that I could glide to about the middle of the Channel where I might be picked up. This idea was quickly frustrated as two 109s attacked and I had to do my very best to avoid them. I turned to defensive tactics, something in which I had been well trained: these tactics consisted of diving at speed and then manoeuvring quickly when they opened fire. Things were getting pretty hairy, especially without my engine power. I thought of jumping out but found that I couldn't open the hood at speed. I knew that my predicament wasn't very good at all. I didn't dare slow down sufficiently to jump as this would have given them an easy shot.

'Fairly quickly we reached ground level, and I think the 109s had run out of ammunition. I saw this big field between two canals as I was coming down and landed my Spitfire with wheels up just short of some tall poplar trees, which caused me a few anxious moments.

The aircraft came to a stop and my first thoughts were to damage the aircraft even more than what it was. I tried to break the instrument panel by kicking it, but try as hard as I could the idea was a failure as the panel was too tough.

'While I was doing this I heard a couple of rifle shots which were a little too close for comfort. I left the aircraft, keeping low down and headed for a nearby farm house. I was very surprised that the shooting continued, still being directed at the aircraft. However by now I was well out of the line of fire. The explanation was that there were patrols on the opposite sides of the two canals. The first chap took a pot shot at me as I was trying to kick in the instrument panel and fortunately missed me. By sheer chance . . . the bullet passed close to the patrol on the other side of the canal.

'The patrol replied by firing back; hence there were several shots fired after I had departed. This was reported to St.Omer HQ; who then accused me of taking up arms after I had surrendered.

This photograph, taken by someone unknown shortly after Joe Kayll was shot down, was sent to England, alerting the RAF to the fact that he was a prisoner of war. [J. Kayll]

Consequently, I was not invited to supper in the Luftwaffe mess as was usual for wing commanders and above.

'I was eventually caught and taken to the interrogation camp at Dulag Luft at Cologne, where after a while I was moved to Spangenberg Castle, which was on top of a hill and surrounded by a dry moat inhabited by wild pigs, which could be relied upon to make considerable noise if disturbed. One day we collected all our old razor blades and some potatoes. Inserting the blades in them we then threw them to the pigs one evening for them to eat. The pigs ate them all and to our absolute amazement they showed no ill effects at all.

'The castle held about 120 POWs, but we had two successful escapes. One man escaped in a laundry basket. Two others got out by posing as members of the Swiss Red Cross who were visiting with a German officer. Both were recaptured within a couple of days. From there we were moved to Warburg, Oflag IX AH, where we met up with the 51st Division under General Fontane. They had been captured intact at St. Valarie. The camp was originally a Hitler Jugend training camp, quite big, holding about two thousand prisoners, and had an entrance at each end, which aided escapers. Various tunnels were dug, with one fatality, who electrocuted himself. A few were successful but no one was out for very long.

'The next move was to a camp in Poland, at Schubin. Just before our move, when half of the camp had gone, an escape was organised by the Army, who had a brilliant electrician. He devised a way of putting all the camp lights out, including the perimeter ones. Four teams with makeshift ladders climbed out over the wire. There were 40 who attempted this escape but only 27 actually escaped, of which three made it to Switzerland, including the organiser, Captain Stallard.

'I was one of those who made good my escape but was recaptured after a week of freedom. I was then sent to Schubin, which had been an Army camp and as such offered potential means of escape. For instance, the lavatory was close to the wire and was used to get about 30 people out. The Germans treated this as a mass escape and as a result guards were put on roads and bridges and all the escapers were recaptured within three or four days. From there we were moved on again, this time to Stalag Luft III, the old compound. We carried on digging tunnels etc. The only one was the Wooden Horse escape, where all three who took part made it to Sweden.'

Wg. Cmdr. Joe Kayll was released in 1945 and returned home to be demobbed. He had been involved in organising escape activity throughout his period of captivity, and he was awarded an OBE for his escape work after his release in May, 1945. He was also mentioned in despatches towards the end of December, 1945.

King George VI presents Joe Kayll with the DSO and DFC for gallantry in France.
[Mrs Valerie Kayll]

On leaving the RAF he worked with two different companies but finally returned to the family timber business. However, it is worth noting that in 1946 he joined the Royal Auxiliary Air Force and commanded 607 Squadron at RAF Ouston, the wheel having turned full circle.

Joe died on 3rd March 2000, aged 85 years – yet another wonderful fighter pilot and a lovely man.

Paddy's War

To my mind any man who was either a pilot or a member of a bomber crew and flew missions against the enemy were brave – in fact very brave. A man who fits this category but was quite a 'card' too is something else. There were certainly many airmen during the war who often lived for the day, and none more so than those who flew during the Battle of Britain in 1940.

I am referring to Wing Commander Patrick 'Paddy' Barthropp, DFC, AFC. Paddy was born in Dublin on 9th November 1920, but educated in England, at Ampleforth College. He started work at Rover Cars. He obtained a short service commission in November 1938 at the age of 18 years and joined 602 (City of Glasgow) Squadron on 8th September 1940, having volunteered to join Fighter Command. His CO was Sqn. Ldr. Sandy Johnstone, an excellent fighter pilot. At this time Paddy had achieved some 22 hours flying Spitfires and was looking forward to joining a squadron who were both flying Spitfires and in combat with the enemy. At the tender age of just 19, he was looking for excitement.

Things didn't get off to a very good start. In September Paddy and his friend Gerald Fisher set off in his clapped-out Austin 7, Henrietta, on a leisurely drive to join his new squadron at Drem, near Edinburgh. It was a very pleasant month weather-wise, and followed a very good summer. The two pilots arrived at Drem and informed the station adjutant that they had come to 'save Britain', a very popular remark. They were thus not too pleased to be told that 602 Squadron had flown down to Tangmere, near Chichester, a week before. Paddy gave a matter of fact shrug of his shoulders, saying that 500 miles-plus was no trouble for Henrietta, Blitzkrieg, his little dachshund (only Paddy could name his pet dog, Blitzkrieg) and young Gerald Fisher. He couldn't help thinking about his travelling expenses of 1d per mile, knowing he would be quite rich by the time they reached the Tangmere airfield.

They finally arrived on Sunday, 8th September, just a couple of weeks after Tangmere had been badly damaged in an attack by a large force of Junkers 87s (Stukas), and the place was an absolute shambles. They were then directed to Westhampnett, a satellite airfield a couple of miles away. There they met their CO and the other members of the squadron.

Paddy had been commissioned and held the rank of pilot officer, as did his friend, Gerald Fisher.

'I spent most of my time either flying in tight formation or as a weaver, which entailed flying behind the squadron and manoeuvring the aircraft from side to side looking for Huns astern. A silk scarf around the neck was a necessity as it stopped the chaffing from the continual twisting and turning of the head. You were inclined to take this task seriously, as you would most likely be the first to be picked off by the enemy in the event of an attack.'

During the first week of his arrival he was well involved in all the action, sometimes flying four sorties a day. He was able to get a close look at the enemy aircraft, including Me109s, Heinkel He111s, Dorniers and Me110s. He often exhausted all his ammunition at the enemy aircraft and happily remarked, 'God knows if I hit anything'.

Paddy Barthropp (right) with Karl Willis (second left) and other members of his mess after being shot down in May 1942. Karl Willis was killed on the eastern front in 1944.

Later in September he was promoted to flying officer. During the early part of October there was no let up and referring to his log book, he flew five sorties in one day. Further reference to the log book reveals entries such as '88s off Pompey', '109 squirted', and '111s damaged'.

'Guy Fawkes Day 1940 is a date I well remember. I took off with 602 on a routine patrol, probably weaving, as weaving was my *métier*, when at 25,000 feet things became hazy and I eventually passed out. I revived at a very low altitude and somehow managed to get down at Warmwell.'

It was later found that three of the four holes of his oxygen plug, feeding air to him, were blocked.

'A normal day during 1940 usually began with us lying around in our Mae Wests at the disposal point waiting for some sort of show to begin. When the alarm sounded we scrambled and once airborne heard through our earphones the instructions, like 'Patrol Mayfield or Tenterden at Angels 25 (meaning 25,000 feet). If you survived the action then in the evening you went off to the local pub, in our case the Unicorn in Chichester, and got pissed, and hopefully hurried home with one of the WAAFs. During one period in August, nearly all the members of 'B' flight caught a dose of crabs, which was not easily cured in those days and considerably cramped one's style, both on the ground and in the air. The usual remedy was to paint the area concerned with gentian violet. However, in the mess one night some bright spark suggested his cure would be to shave a narrow channel down the centre of the pubic hairs from the stomach to the penis, then set fire to one side and shoot the little bastards as they ran across.

'On a more serious note I, like many others, was privileged to have known, fought and drunk with people like Bob Tuck, Johnnie Johnson, Killy Kilmartin, Jim Hallowes, Sailor Malan, Brian Kingcome, Douglas Bader and Bob Oxspring. They embodied for me the type of leadership we required at this time.'

Paddy was posted from 602 to 610 Squadron in the December, while his old squadron returned to Scotland. He stayed for only two months and in February 1941, he was posted to 91 Squadron at Hawkinge in Kent. This is where his war took on a more serious note, as his duties changed considerably. It included flying in pairs across the Channel shadowing enemy formations, ship and troop movements and, to a certain extent, the deployment of enemy fighters in the Pas de Calais area. There were several flamboyant pilots in the 'Jim Crow' Squadron, the leader being 27-year-old Paddy Green, a Cambridge blue. Also there was Johannes Jacobus Le Roux, known as Chris – a very good-looking guy who, Paddy said, always got the best-looking girls. Chris and Paddy often flew together as 'Hurdle 8 and 9', and off duty they were very good friends, drinking together and hunting the female species.

'One day in April,' Paddy recalls, 'Chris and I set off on a "rhubarb", which defined meant, "shoot up anything you see that happens to be around".

'Just off Boulogne was a bunch of German pongos (soldiers) laying barbed wire traps nearly half a mile out in the shallows at low tide, and for the first time in the war I had a tinge of sadness for the helpless soldiers who provided such an excellent target for 16 perfectly aimed machine guns. There were no survivors.'

'Chris' Le Roux, a South African pilot with 91 Squadron, standing in front of Spitfire VB in the summer of 1941.

105

RAF Hawkinge, 1941. Left to right: Orange O'Meara, Sgt. Olly Cooper, Tony Lee Knight, Paddy Barthropp, Sgt. Goodwin, Chris Le Roux.

Chris Le Roux had the unique experience of being shot down twelve times but accumulated a score of downing 24 enemy aircraft. Sadly he went missing over the Channel later in the war.

In June Paddy deviously acquired a superb two-litre Lagonda from a local scrap metal dealer for 400 gallons of high octane fuel, which was liberally dispersed around Hawkinge in four gallon drums. (This car, which he still has, is now worth £40,000.) Some of the airmen fitted a 25-gallon tank under the back seat of the car so that he had plenty of fuel. The snag was that, apart from being used illegally, it was coloured bright green. The way around that problem was to fit a further tank (a small one near the carburettor) that would house half a gallon of legal fuel in case it was checked by the special investigation branch, as often happened. The flyers even had a way of warning each other of an imminent inspection. A message on the tannoy system would announce, 'Will corporal Austin or Morris report to the duty pilot immediately'. They certainly knew how to organise matters.

Towards the end of August, he was on the move again, this time to 610 Squadron as a flight commander and based at his old stamping ground, Westhampnett. Once again his duties were slightly changed, and he took part in many sweeps and patrols over northern France. In the early stages of this move he felt uncomfortable with his situation, and he met disaster on 27th August.

'I was leading a flight on a "circus" at 26,000 feet over the St. Omer region. We were bounced by Me109s and the ensuing debacle saw my no. 2, Sgt. Ballard, blown out of the sky. I am sure that the 'B' Flight pilots, who had more experience than me in this type of operation, blamed me for what happened. This catastrophe has always haunted me. It was a relief when we were all sent to Leconfield for a rest.'

One evening some of the pilots went to the Beverley Arms in the centre of Leconfield. They noticed that there were some comfortable looking chairs in the bar, and rather more than was necessary. Their mess, on the other hand, had only three, so they stacked a few into the back of Paddy's Lagonda. Unfortunately, on their way back to their base they were stopped by a number of police and questioned about the chairs. One of this number was 'a superior- looking man with scrambled egg on his cap and wearing a greatcoat'. Paddy called him a conscientious objector, among other things, but somehow they were allowed to continue their journey back to base.

The next day, the station commander, Tim Morice called Paddy to his office. When he arrived he was introduced to the man he had encountered the evening before and had called various unpleasant names. He got quite a shock when he noticed on his chest a number of medals, including the DSO and bar, the MC and MM from the 1914–18 war. He was the chief constable of East Riding. Poor Paddy was so ashamed that he didn't know where to look. However, the story has a pleasant ending, as they became good friends and Paddy was often invited to his house for dinner.

During September 1941 he received a letter from Jamie Rankin telling him that he had been awarded the DFC, but it would be another five months before his investiture.

Around August 1942 was possibly Paddy's worst and unluckiest time. On St. Patrick's Day he had to take part in a formation flypast for a new intake of pupils. He was one of a group of three, and as they came around at about 300ft, three aircraft with Polish pilots appeared flying in the opposite direction. There was a mighty crash as two aircraft hit head-on. Parts of the crashing aircraft tore a gash in the side of Paddy's aircraft and he was lucky not to have been killed: he later said that he felt safer flying a combat mission. Then that same evening Paddy wrote off his beloved Lagonda after colliding with a taxi cab in Knightsbridge.

On the 28th April he was summoned to Brentford court where he was fined £2 for 'assault and battery' against the licensee of a pub in Hounslow. They say things happen in threes: well, perhaps Paddy would be ok after this.

It was now May 1942, and once again he was off to another squadron. This time his posting was 122 Squadron, based at Hornchurch. He arrived there on the 12th May in his newly acquired drophead Rover, a 21st birthday present. His duties now included the odd convoy patrol with 'A' Flight. By this time he was already a very successful fighter pilot, having completed 317 missions for the loss of one Lysander and two badly holed Spitfires, a very successful fighter pilot. What he didn't know at this stage, however, was that he wasn't going to fly many more operational flights.

Five days after his arrival he flew escort with many other Spitfires escorting six Boston bombers on a mission to bomb a paint factory at Audruicq, close to St.Omer airfield. He hated crossing the Channel. Jim Hallowes, a top fighter pilot, had given him some very good advice, which was never to break away from the formation.

'Around 20,000 feet,' Paddy wrote later, 'we were attacked by Focker Wulf 190s, a type I hadn't seen before. Two of them, flown by Hauptman's Karl Willius and Rolf Hermichen, appeared from nowhere. In the process of dispatching Hermichen to his ancestors, Willius got behind me, letting me have it forcibly with his 20mm canons that removed the bottom part of the rudder bar and the control column. There was no alternative but to bale out, praying silently that Mr. Irvin's magic silk device would function effectively. In a way, I suppose, it can be said that it did.

'Although my parachute opened correctly, my worries were far from over. Willius followed me down, doing dummy attacks, trying to collapse the canopy, and as I had previously witnessed pilots being shot at while making a parachute descent I really thought I was a goner. It was a beautiful day and below I could see little figures in uniform converging towards my anticipated point of arrival. The landing wasn't one of

my best. I hit the roof of a barn, crashing to the concrete floor below. Having seen my free fall display onto his barn, a French farmer appeared. I just had time to hand over to him the francs that had been provided for use in the eventuality of escape, together with my parachute. Then the dreaded Wermacht were entering the scene in force.

'An irate and nervous officer stuck a .38 revolver to my forehead and I was truly convinced that he was going to shoot me. Fortunately, it was only to keep me quiet whilst one of his chums searched me. They took my gold half hunter watch, a 21st birthday present, and my silver cigarette case. I was then driven in a Standard 8 to a large terraced house in the small town of Audruicq and there locked up in the loft. I took stock of my injuries and, except for a very sore back resulting in my fall and a few shrapnel splinters in one leg, everything was in working order.

'That evening Hauptman Karl Willius, who prior to hostilities had been at Cambridge, paid me a visit and I told him my thoughts about his bloody feigned onslaughts during my parachute drop. He was extremely angry, and I could see that I had offended him. But later, after a friendly chat which included discussing the merits of the Spitfire versus Messerschmitt in combat, he asked if I had any complaints and I mentioned my watch and case. He mumbled something to the effect that the German pongos were much the same as ours and departed.

'Later that evening one of his NCO's appeared with my watch, my cigarette case filled, some black pudding and bottles of lager beer.

The following day, Karl, with four of his fellow henchmen, came and took me to their airfield at St.Omer where we discussed the futility of war and smoked copious cigarettes.'

Life in the loft was pretty grim, the food meagre and so the food and drink given to Paddy by Willius was very welcome. With an armed guard outside the door and a 50ft drop to the concrete ground outside, escaping wasn't an option. Apart from the fact that it was every officer's duty at least to try, Paddy was desperate to escape – he wasn't born to be a caged animal. – but he had to bide his time .

He spent about two weeks in the loft, but one day a young officer together with an escort arrived and took him to St. Omer railway station where he travelled through France and into Germany. It was night time as he reached Cologne, the first stop, on 30th May 1942.

As he arrived, the air raid sirens sounded. He was roughly hand-cuffed by his left arm and right leg underneath a large wrought iron railway seat. The escorts disappeared, leaving him extremely frightened and on his own as everyone else rushed to the shelters. On this day 868 aircraft dropped a total of 1,455 bombs on Cologne, two-thirds of them incendiary bombs. German records show that 2,500 separate fires were started. Some 12,000 buildings were hit, more than 3,000 totally destroyed.

Paddy was extremely lucky. Although it felt to him as if he were the target, the bombs didn't fall close to the railway station. There was dust and broken glass all around him, however, and the noise was deafening, his fear difficult to describe. He remembers a woman bending down and in English wishing him good luck. He would continue to have nightmares about this particular night for the rest of his life.

How the Daily Express reported the raid on Cologne.

The next morning he continued his journey to Frankfurt-on-Main and entered his first POW camp, where he was interrogated. In June he was moved to probably the most famous POW camp in the world, Stalag Luft III, near Sagan – scene of the Great Escape'.

He wasn't about to sit still and await the end of the war, however, and was soon involved in the various escape tunnels and other methods of escape. Paddy was, as could be expected, a trouble maker – a 'pain in the butt' to the Germans. After one incident he was frogmarched through the camp with Tex Ash and out into the nearby woods. They were ordered to kneel down and, in his words, 'I never prayed so hard in my life'.

It must have worked. They were ordered to stand, and were then marched back into camp and given 28 days in the 'cooler'. One of the best known guards at the camp was Feldwebel Glemnitz, and after the war he came to England and stayed at Paddy's home. (They both appeared on the This is your Life programme for Wings Day, the British commander in the camp.)

Later Paddy was moved to another camp, Oflag XXXIB, which was near to Schubin in Poland. He was soon involved in yet another tunneling plan. Before the breakout he had learned that a Heinkel He111 had been forced down in Yugoslavia, and the plan was that six of them, moving in pairs, would meet up with this aircraft and fly to the Middle East. On the afternoon of the break-out 32 POWs were shut into the tunnel, cramped head to toe, remaining in that position for nearly five hours.

'The stench was unbearable,' Paddy recalled later, 'and I will always remember the rush of fresh air when Tex Ash and Eddie Asselin broke through the last few feet of earth and into the open.'

Two crews, one Polish and the other Czech, managed to get to Warsaw, to an address they had been given, but they were never heard of again. Two others were drowned crossing the water to Sweden.

Paddy escaped from the camp with Wilf Wise and made it to a town called Hohensalza, a good distance away, only to be apprehended by the Gestapo and taken to their headquarters. This was a frightening time, and after some intense interrogation they were paraded outside in front of German troops and Hitler Youth.

'One youth said to me in English, "Hitler is a good man and Churchill is a very bad man". My answer was a little unflattering to the Fuhrer, whereupon the youth spat at me, followed by several others.'

In the winter of 1944 he was back at Stalag Luft III, but on 28th January the prisoners were ordered to get ready to move out. The Russians were approaching, and the Germans thought that POWs might be useful as hostages at a later stage. They were forced to endure several long marches in snow storms and freezing weather, with little or no food.

With the end of the war Paddy returned to England in a Lancaster bomber and landed at Wing, near Aylesbury. (It was tragic that the first Lancaster to take off carrying POWs back to England crashed, and that all on board lost their lives.) To this day Paddy is still fighting to get the third of his RAF pay that was deducted while he was a POW.

His civvy life was just as exciting as his service career. He started off with three weeks official leave and four weeks unofficial leave. He was left an inheritance from an aunt who had died shortly after he became a POW. A large amount of this money disappeared in various clubs in London, including Vanity Fair Club, Mayfair Club and many more. He liked fast cars and even faster ladies. He did various jobs, including being a jockey, before returning to the RAF for a short while. When he left the RAF as a wing commander in 1957 he set up a high class limousine hire firm with another ex-pilot, his good friend Brian Kingcome.

His humorous wonderfully written book *Paddy* was first published in 1986 (ISBN 0 7030 0325 9) but has had several reprints. There is a lot more to Patrick Peter Colum 'Paddy' Barthropp than I have space to tell. He calls a spade a spade, and is a man so transparently honest that you either like or dislike him. Me, I not only like the guy but I have the greatest respect for him. In my eyes he is a star, and a pretty big one at that. I am privileged to call him a friend.

Halifax Crash at Lewes

In April 1943 Stirlings, Halifaxes, Wellingtons and Lancaster bombers from all of 33 squadrons took part in massive attacks on the Ruhr and several other important targets, one of which was the Skoda armaments factory at Pilzen. In bright moonlight, most crews mistook an asylum building 11 kilometres from the factory as their target. As if this wasn't enough, the Luftwaffe came upon the main force and was responsible for most of the 36 crews reported as missing. This was one of Bomber Command's worst nights, as a further 18 aircraft failed to return from an operation to Mannheim. The scourge of the German night-fighters had been in evidence earlier in April, but this was a particularly successful night for them.

One of the aircraft taking part in the Pilzen raid was a Halifax II no. DT791 ZA-K, of 10 Squadron, its pilot being Flt. Lt. Johnny Wood.

Halifax II no. DT 791 ZA-K, call sign K-Kitty, with its crew at its base at Melbourne, Yorkshire. It came down at Lewes in Sussex. [Bob Elliston]

They had attended their briefing and were dreading the flight to Pilzen, a long and difficult trip to a city that was heavily defended. At 8.44 pm on Friday, 16th April the aircraft taxied along the runway at RAF Melbourne in Yorkshire and they were on their way. A total of 327 bombers were tasked for this one raid, while another 271 attacked Mannheim.

The crew of K for Kitty settled back for the long flight, their eyes scanning the skies for enemy aircraft. They were carrying four 1,000-pound bombs and one of 500 pounds. They dropped them from a height of 8,000 feet, but were about seven miles off target. In a complicated plan, the main force had been ordered to confirm the position of the Skoda factory visually, the pathfinder markers being intended only as a general guide. In the event only six crews brought back photographs which showed that they were within three miles of their intended target and the Skoda factory was not hit at all. One official report states that 200 German soldiers were killed when their barracks near the asylum was bombed.

On their way home the Halifax was hit in the outer port engine by flak, and further damage was caused as they reached the French coast, when the port inner engine was also hit. It was only the flying skill of the pilot that allowed the aircraft to manage crossing the Channel. They made landfall near Seaford in Sussex and followed the River Ouse searching for a place to land, but they crashed on the Landport allotments, close to the Offham Road at Lewes, where the fuselage broke in two pieces. It was 5.23am.

Of the eight-man crew, only the pilot was uninjured. They were helped from their burning aircraft by members of the 3rd Canadian Light A.A. who were manning a Bofors gun site by the Bastion, about 200 yards from the crash. They were ably assisted by members of the public living in the nearby houses, who then made tea for the rescuers. The police report states that when the police and fire brigade arrived the aircraft was well on fire but was extinguished in a short while. The crew were lying on the bank. They were taken on stretchers to the Victoria Hospital nearby, some of them unconscious. Since the hospital had only a skeleton staff on duty, the police were involved in getting several doctors and nurses to the hospital, while two constables helped remove the men's heavy flying clothing in order to assess the seriousness of their injuries. Several of the men stayed in hospital for the next few days with broken bones. They were all discharged at a later date, returned to their base at Melbourne and allocated to different aircraft.

The remains of the Halifax were examined. It was classed as 'E' category – unfit to be repaired – and removed on a low loader a few days later. Before it went an unknown youth took a photograph of it on the allotments. He must have had a friend who developed the film, as taking photographs of military objects was illegal. The photograph is reproduced below.

The official figures for the raid were:

Killed 200
POWs 51
Evaded capture 11
Injured 8

A further 28 airmen with 408 (Canadian) Squadron lost their lives during this raid.

The crashed Halifax on the allotments at Lewes. [Bob Elliston]

Sadly two members of the Halifax crew failed to survive the war. Sgt. Percy O'Kill died on 7th September 1943 when his aircraft was shot down by a night-fighter over Germany. He was still a member of 10 Squadron and his Halifax II, no. JDI66 ZA-G, was on an operation to Munich. The aircraft crashed at Kaufbeuren with two members killed and the others becoming POWs. He was buried in the local cemetery, but in 1945 his remains were removed to Durnbach war cemetery.

The air bomber, PO Cyril Stepney, was also killed during a bombing mission. He was promoted to flying officer and transferred to 35 Squadron, based at Graveley, Huntingdon. His Halifax, no.HR676 -TL-V was shot down while on an operation to Mannheim during the night of 18/19th November 1943. The aircraft crashed at Mertloch, about 9km south-east of Mayen. All seven members of the crew were killed. His body was buried at Mertloch cemetery but later re-interred at Rheinberg British military cemetery.

The navigator, PO Kenneth Whynes, died in 1983, while the pilot, Flt. Lt. Johnny Wood died in 1987.

The 1943 Barcombe Bomber

The night of 29/30th May 1943 was a clear one, with very good visibility and patchy cloud formations around 20,000 feet. That was the sort of weather facing Flt.Lt. John Lintott, a pilot in 'B' Flight of 85 Squadron based at West Malling in Kent. At around 12.30am he took off for night practice with his operator, Sgt. Gilling-Lax, GC, in a Mosquito XII night-fighter. They were under the control of Flt. Lt. Parker, the controller at RAF Watling.

After a series of practice runs they were instructed to gain height to 25,000 feet and were advised of an enemy aircraft about seven miles from their position. They were-vectored and informed that the enemy aircraft was at a height of some 27,000 feet and crossing from port to starboard north-west of their current position.

The crew of the Junkers which crashed at Barcombe, near Lewes. The observer, Oberlt. Alfred Stanke, is second from the left. [John Dibley]

Initial contact was made at a range of a little over three miles. John Lintott manouvered until he was dead astern and slightly below his quarry, which he initially mistook as a Dornier Do 217: he could only make out the exhausts coming from the rear of the plane and positive indentfication was difficult against the dark night sky. It was, in fact, a Junkers Ju88, and the pilot was flying on a dead level course, unaware of the Mosquito stalking him.

Flt. Lt. John Lintott, pilot of the Mosquito which shot down the Barcombe bomber.

Lintott closed on the enemy aircraft until he was just 500 feet behind and slightly below – a classic attacking position. At this stage, the enemy aircraft was sighted from the ground over Sussex, about five miles north of Lewes. He opened fire and scored straight away, the starboard engine bursting into flames. That was probably the first the German crew knew about the Mosquito attacking them. A second burst of machine gun fire set the port engine alight. A further two or three bursts of fire struck the enemy aircraft, and shortly afterwards it began to lose height, making a gentle diving turn to port. Lintott orbitted and at the same time contacted RAF Watling and Biggin Hill while watching the enemy aircraft going down. Seconds later the enemy aircraft broke up in mid-air, and blazing pieces of aircraft fell to earth.

No evasive action was taken by the German pilot and no return fire was aimed at the Mosquito, which returned to its base at 2.30am. What had not been noticed or even mentioned in Lintott's report was the fact that the German crew had baled out. They landed in the Sussex countryside and were soon rounded up.

The larger part of the enemy aircraft, Junkers Ju88S-1, (no. 140550) of 1/KG66 landed in a 20-acre field known as Lea Shade on Longfield Farm, Barcombe. The pilot, Oberfw. Seigfried Simon landed in Newick Park and surrendered. He was then taken to Lewes police station, arriving at 3.45am.

Fw. Paul Korte, the wireless operator, suffered a fractured ankle and was taken to the Canadian hospital at Smallfields. Oberlt. Alfred Stanke, the observer, landed at Bevington Farm, Five Ash Down and was captured by the occupant, William Grant. He was handed over to the police in Uckfield and he, too, was subsequently taken to Lewes police station.

There were 18 unexploded bombs still in the fuselage of the enemy plane, and these were difused by an RAF bomb disposal unit. The aircraft was guarded by members 'C' Coy. 18th Home Guard, Isfield, together with Pc. Wilkinson and special constables based at Barcombe. They were later relieved by members of the Queen's Regiment based in Lewes

The two German prisoners, Simon and Stanke, were taken by train to an unknown destination, arranged by the RAF. The remains of the Junkers 88 was later removed by the maintenance unit and taken to Faygate.

Alfred Stanke, the observer of the Junkers, who became a prisoner of war. [John Dibley]

Best of Them All

This is the story of possibly the best fighter pilot of them all during the Battle of Britain, a man fanatical about killing the enemy. He had seen slaughter and terror in his homeland during and after the invasion of Czechoslovakia by Germany at the beginning of the Second World War. He left his country determined to do his part in bringing peace and freedom to his country and others.

Josef Frantisek was born in Otaslavice, Czechoslovakia on 7th October 1912. He joined the Czech Air Force in the mid 1930s and it was obvious to his instructors that he would be a pilot of exceptional qualities. He passed all of his examinations and tests with top marks, his flying abilities having eclipsed his instructor's expectations.

Josef Frantisek, who destroyed 17 enemy aircraft. Having survived being shot down in action over Beachy Head in on 9th September 1940, he was killed the following October.

When the Germans invaded his country he could see that his country stood little chance of defeating their superior forces. He decided that his best course of action was to go to Poland and fight from there. On his way he attacked and killed a column of German troops before flying off to Poland. He joined the Polish Air Force and, although it cannot be now confirmed, destroyed several German aircraft. Then Germany invaded Poland and, once again, he was forced to leave the country.

He escaped to Romania, where he was interned, but he soon escaped and made his way to France. His route was arduous, via the Balkans and Syria. Arrived in France in May 1940, he joined a French fighter squadron and soon showed his great prowess by destroying 11 enemy aircraft in a short space of time. He picked up his first award, the French Croix de Guerre, for his courageous actions.

After the collapse of France he made his way to England, converted to Hurricanes and joined 303 Squadron. This squadron was formed on 22nd July 1940 at Northolt and equipped with Hurricane 1s. He held the rank of sergeant pilot (service no. 793451)

The pilots worked hard during their training period and suffered a number of crash-landings and other minor mishaps. However, at this time a number of Hurricanes had to be written off due to accidents. Around this time a number of other Polish squadrons were being formed as more and more Polish pilots made their way to England in order to take part in the war against their enemies.

Josef was very soon in the middle of the action, as was expected, but although the squadron flew many sorties they had to wait until 30th August before enjoying their first success. On this day, a Friday, waves of German aircraft came flooding across the Channel around 10am. The weather was fair, with good visibility across the Channel. There were about 50 enemy bombers and a large fighter escort.

The combat took place east of Dungerness, and the squadron claimed two bombers destroyed and two Me 110s damaged. The following day the squadron made its first operation at full strength, with 13 Hurricanes in the air. Josef was desperate to open his account with his new squadron and latched onto a Me109E and chased it across the Channel, giving up the chase only when he was warned off by anti-aircraft fire over the French coast. He was furious at one getting away.

On the 2nd September he and Sgt. Jan Rogowski were flying as 'tail-end Charlies' when they spotted Me109s diving out of the sun. They turned to meet the enemy head-on. This was when Josef was able to claim his first enemy aircraft, shooting it down into the sea. The wounded German pilot was rescued by his own side. However Josef began to wonder just whose side he was on when he was shot at first by a Spitfire in the early patrol and later in the day by a Hurricane. Fortunately his aircraft wasn't damaged or he injured.

He scored again the following day, two more on the 5th and another on the 6th September. This was 'more like it', he said to himself. The 9th September almost saw his demise, as he was attacked by two Me109s, while pursuing an enemy bomber. Another pilot, FO Jan Zumbach, said in a written report, 'When we saw the bombers and the Me's which were fighting with the Hurricanes and Spitfires, I saw a bomber being attacked by Josef's Hurricane. This Hurricane was being attacked by two 109's and escaped into cloud.'

Josef claimed one Me109 and one Heinkel He111, but his Hurricane no. P3975- RF-U was badly shot up and he was forced to make a crash- landing on the outskirts of Brighton.

'When we arrived in sight of the Germans,' he later reported, 'swarms of Me109s dived from a great height to attack us. I saw one Me109 going in to attack a Hurricane in front of me. I attacked it starboard to beam, firing at 150/100 yards at the engine, which began to burn. He tried to escape by climbing, and I saw him open the cockpit preparatory to jumping. I shot at the cockpit and the pilot collapsed. The enemy aircraft fell in flames to the ground [Horsham area]. I then saw a Hurricane in flames and the pilot jumped.'

The pilot who baled out was Sgt. Kazimierz Wunsche, aged 21, who landed at Portslade. He had been seriously wounded in the back and arms and was taken to Hove Hospital. It would be several

months before he was able to return to the squadron. His Hurricane, P3700 RF-E, crashed at Saddlescombe Farm at Poynings, a write-off. A 'dig' took place in 1979, when a few parts of the aircraft were recovered.

'A Spitfire came down to circle around the pilot,' Josef continued. 'I went for a He111, and two Me109s attacked me. I hid in cloud at about 17,000 feet for seven minutes – I played hide and seek with them in the cloud. During a right turn I came out of the cloud and saw in front of me,

Kazimierz Wunsche.

about 10 yards away, and also coming out of the cloud, a He111. I very nearly collided with it, and fired at the front of the fuselage at an angle of 45 degrees from above and behind. The front of the enemy aircraft fell to pieces with the cockpit and both engines in flames. I do not know if this enemy aircraft fell on the ground or in the sea, owing to the clouds. As I broke away one Me109 attacked me from above and another from below.

'I hid again in the clouds and flew towards France to keep under cover. Over the Channel I climbed out of cloud and was hit by four

Me shells, one in the port wing, one through the left tank, which did not catch fire, one through the radiator. It is only owing to the armour plating behind me that the fourth shell didn't kill me. Two Spitfires came to my rescue, and shot down the Me109, which apparently was the one which had hit me. I saw the damage which had been done, and was obliged to find a landing place as the engine temperature was mounting dangerously.

On a little hill north–east of Brighton [this was at Woodingdean, close to the Downs Hotel] I found a field of cabbages and made an excellent landing. The police came immediately – not only did they not make any difficulties, but were very kind to me. They anchored the Hurricane, shut off the petrol and oxygen and left the plane guarded by a policeman. They took me by car to Brighton, and I returned to Northolt by train. Sergeant Wunsche's parachute was at the police station. I brought mine home.

'At the railway station the people were very kind to me. Girls gave me some chocolate and people photographed me. I am very grateful for the kindness which was shown to me by everyone.'

Josef felt few effects from this incident. Two days later three more enemy aircraft fell to his guns.

September was a good month for him. On the 15th a Me 110 went down somewhere between south London and Hastings. On the 18th a Me109 fell to his guns over West Malling. On Friday 20th September 1940 he was decorated with the DFM by King George VI at RAF Northolt. Early in the afternoon of Thursday 26th September King George VI visited Northolt again, and after visiting the Canadian no.1 Squadron, also inspected the famous Polish Squadron. All the airmen were lined up for his inspection and the king shook hands with many of them, exchanging a few words. He then signed the first volume of the illustrated squadron chronicle. As the royal visit was coming to an end, they were scrambled at 4.10pm to the Guildford area to catch raiders attacking Portsmouth. Josef was among these pilots and was flying Hurricane no. R4175 RF-R. He claimed downing two He111s and chasing his second bomber over France

'I shot an enemy aircraft down,' he said 'and he fell to earth in France. It was then that I noticed that I was over France, and turned and flew back to Northolt.'

This Heinkel He111 was probably the one from 3/KG55 that force-landed at Dreux after combat with fighters over Portsmouth. Two members of the crew were wounded, namely Oblt. Karbe and Lt. Wilser, and the aircraft was 40 per cent damaged.

The following day he destroyed a Me 110 over Gatwick and a He111 over Horsham while flying the same aircraft as the previous day. On the last day of September he claimed two more enemy planes, one destroyed and a probable, both in the Brooklands area.

The squadron took off early on a routine patrol over Biggin Hill on Tuesday 8th October with Josef flying Hurricane no. V4175 RF-R, one of 12 aircraft from the squadron. On the way back to Northolt, at about 9.40am, he suddenly left the formation. He failed to answer any calls on his RT and crashed at Cuddington Way, Ewell, in Surrey. It is thought that his oxygen system had failed.

Josef was killed in the crash. The squadron mourned the loss of a brilliant fighter pilot, who is buried in Northwood cemetery in Middlesex.

During the Battle of Britain he was credited with a total of 17 enemy aircraft destroyed and one probable. This made him the highest scoring pilot during the Battle of Britain – a little known fact.

A much decorated pilot, he was awarded the Virtuti Militari (5th class) on 23rd December 1940, the Krzyz Walecznych and three Bars on 1st February 1941 and the Czech Military Cross on 15 July 1941

Josef Frantisek's gravestone,
in Northwood cemetery.

A Belgian Pilot's Story

The clock showed 11.08am on Monday 29th. March 1943 as four Focker Wulf 190s from 10 Staffel Jagdgeschwader 54 came in fast and low over the Channel for an attack on Brighton.

One of these aircraft was flown by 21-year-old Obergefreiter Joachim Koch, who strafed the streets with machine gun and canon fire. This scattered many of the people who were caught outside, although fortunately no one suffered serious injury. The German fighter-bombers then dropped their large bombs on the town.

One fell near the corner of William Street and Carlton Hill, striking the top part of a house at an angle. This, in turn, deflecting it into a position almost parallel with the ground, made it into something resembling a torpedo. Travelling at speed, it entered an open first floor window at the southern end of the fruit and vegetable market in Circus Street and continued through the whole length of the building, killing one of the employees. It struck the north wall of the building, bursting through and showering the roadway and pavement with debris.

It is incredible that the bomb failed to explode at this point. The collision with the wall reduced its speed, and it now crossed Sussex Street and struck the Brighton municipal clinic on the corner of Ivory Place. It exploded just to the west of the entrance hall in one of the main offices. This bomb killed and injured a number of people, including children.

Although, generally, these types of attacks lasted but a few minutes, information about incoming enemy aircraft was being continually updated at RAF operations rooms and transmitted via the chain home radar stations. As a result of this information, Spitfires from 610 Squadron, stationed at Biggin Hill, had been scrambled and were soon on their way to intercept the enemy aircraft.

One of the Spitfires was flown by FO Francois Veneseon. After the attack on Brighton orders were to attack Hove on the way out, and as they started their westward journey the approaching Spitfires were spotted. Whether it was panic or not, one of the Fw190s – the one flown by Koch – suddenly turned south-wards, crossing the coastline just to the east of the Palace Pier in a south-westerly direction. He was chased by Veneseon's Spitfire. As they cleared the coast a short burst from the Spitfire Vb was enough: it spelled the end for the FW 190 and for Koch, as they crashed into the sea some 500 yards south of the Palace Pier with a very large splash. The FW 190 (no. 2576) soon sank and Koch's body was washed up on the beach about a month later, on Sunday 25th.April, at Ovingdean. He is buried in the cemetery in Bear Road, Brighton.

FLYER BIOG

Francois Veneseon, born on 19th October 1920, was of Belgian nationality. He was a pupil pilot in the 80e Promotion intake on 1st March 1939 but was 'washed out' on 25th May. He then became a corporal air gunner with IIIe Group/2e Regiment at Nivelles on Fox VICs, but on 13th May 1940 he escaped to France as his country was being overrun. He sailed on the MS Effrick from St. Jean-de-Luz, reaching England on 23rd June 1940. Here on 19th August he joined 235 Squadron as an air-gunner on Blenheim fighters based at both Thorney Island and Bircham Newton.

On 20th November he was posted to 272 Squadron, but was then accepted for pilot training, attending 13 SFTS. He was awarded a DFC on 21st December 1942.

During August 1940 Veneseon was a sergeant, flying Blenheim fighters on coastal patrol duties. He was commissioned in July, 1941 and in November was posted to 350 (Belgian) Squadron in the Western Desert. He returned to England to fly Spitfires.

On the 19th. August, 1942, he made his first claim over Dieppe, destroying two Fw190s. He later had a share in shooting down a Junkers Ju 52. In early 1943 he was promoted to flying officer and posted to 610 Squadron. He later had a half share in destroying a Me110 over Cap St. Mathieu.

Early in 1944, he returned to 350 Squadron as a flight commander, having been decorated with the DFC.

On D-Day, 6th June 1944, his Spitfire suffered an engine failure, causing him to crash near the unit's airfield at Friston, Sussex, and he was killed.

A Ditched Halifax

This is the story of a Halifax aircraft on a bombing mission to Germany. The captain and pilot, Flt. Sgt, Sam Liggett, tells it from his own notes and his memory. It relates the flight from England, the damage received, the attack by a Messerschmitt Me 110, and finally the ditching in the sea at Seaford, East Sussex.

The crew consisted of the following airmen: -

Flt Sgt. Sam Liggett	'Skip'	pilot
Sgt. Len Trowbridge	'Len'	navigator
Sgt. Bill Watt	'Bill'	bomb aimer
Sgt. John Birrell	'Jock'	wireless operator
Sgt. Eric Gosling	'Ginge	flight engineer
Sgt. Keith Smith	'Lofty'	tail gunner
Sgt. Leslie Hughes	'Tich'	mid upper gunner

No 78 Squadron was based at RAF Breighton in Yorkshire, and during the late evening of Friday 9th. July 1943 the crews were called for briefing. As they wandered into the room, thoughts turned to the target for that night's mission. It was almost a certainty that it would involve a flight to Germany, but where exactly?

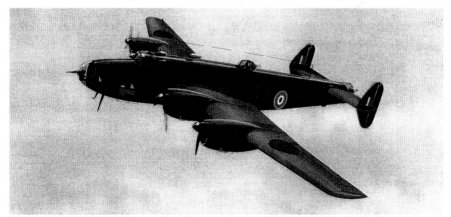

Painting by a sergeant of 78 squadron of the Halifax ditched at Seaford by Sam Liggett. [S. Liggett]

They settled into their seats, and before long it was announced that the target for tonight was Gelsenkirchen. It was to be a big raid, with 418 aircraft taking part. This number was to comprise 218 Lancaster bombers, 190 Halifax bombers and 10 Mosquito aircraft from many squadrons – Lancasters from 9, 12 and 50 Squadrons, Halifaxes from 51, 78 and 102 Squadrons and 10 Mosquitoes as pathfinders. They were wished good luck and, with the words of the briefing ringing in their ears, they made for their aircraft.

By 11.05 the aircraft were given the green light and were taxiing

Sam Liggett in 1943. [S. Liggett]

along the runway. All were making for the point where they would meet and set course for their target. Sam Liggett himself now takes up the story:

'We had a pretty uneventful trip across, each one of us being pretty well occupied with our own jobs until we got near to the target. The searchlights were all around and the flak was very heavy. I thought at one stage we were doing pretty well, and then they got us coned. I knew that somehow I had to get the plane out of these searchlights and I did just about everything I could. They were so bright, it was almost like daylight. I continued to try to evade them, when all of a sudden we got hit.

'The flak had made a bit of a mess on the port wing. At that initial stage we couldn't quite see the extent of the damage. The inner engine then caught fire. By this time it was pretty bumpy and the flak continued to be all around us. Ginger and I were able to feather the engine and then extinguish the fire. We were feeling quite lucky at this stage. We knew we had the damage and, considering, the plane was flying quite well. Shortly after this bit of excitement we found that some of the fuel tanks had been hit and badly holed. This is just what we didn't want; we needed all the fuel we had on board. Ginger checked and re-checked the fuel gauges, but unfortunately there was no mistake, the fuel tanks had been holed. All this and we hadn't yet reached the target.

'However, it wasn't long before we were close, and as we started to run into the target Bill ordered the bomb doors to be opened. This was readily done and now everything was ready: it would now be just a very short while before dropping our bombs and then we could turn for home, home sweet home.

'The next few minutes were just so unbelievable, it was a real rough ride, and it was something like you read about but don't really believe. We were flying between the other aircraft slipstreams and the ack ack fire was all around very close to our aircraft. We really didn't want any more damage. It was a pretty grim ride and quite difficult to keep the plane flying straight and on a steady course, but soon it was all over.

'Bill called "Bombs away!", and as they left the plane there was some relief, and we then turned for home. I selected "bomb doors

Keith 'Lofty' Smith, the Halifax tail gunner. He later transferred to the pathfinder force and was killed over the Ruhr on 20th December 1943. [S. Liggett]

closed", but they remained open. The hand pump was tried but they still would not close. This could be a problem, for two reasons: one, the aircraft speed would be reduced and secondly, we had to cross the Channel. Now we couldn't afford to come down on water. With one of the engines out and the bomb doors open, speed was reduced, and to a degree we could be a sitting duck for any enemy aircraft that wished to attack us. We all knew the situation, and so we all kept our eyes peeled for any sign of enemy aircraft.

'We knew that there was every chance that we might be attacked, although hoping that we wouldn't. The time ticked past as we got ever nearer to the Channel and home. We had got settled on our home course and things were going OK when, about 15 minutes later, Lofty, the tail gunner, called out that a Messerschmitt Me 110 was approaching from the starboard side.

At this time we were flying at approx. 17,000 feet with clear visibility. The time was then 0200hrs, this plane was about 500 yards away and coming in to attack.'

The following is copied from the official report, submitted by the rear gunner, Sgt Keith Smith, and the mid upper gunner, Sgt. Leslie Hughes:

'Monica [warning frequency system] gave the first warning and a few seconds later the rear gunner saw an Me110 down on starboard quarter at a range of approx. 500 yards coming up to attack. Enemy aircraft immediately opened fire and put rear turret out of action, luckily not injuring gunner. Pilot turned sharply to starboard on rear gunner's instructions and then commenced to corkscrew. Enemy aircraft made four attacks from the port quarter level and the mid upper gunner got in several bursts. In the fourth attack the mid upper gunner saw the enemy's port engine burst into flames. The enemy aircraft came in for a fifth attack and the mid upper gunner got in a burst at a 100-yard range and also raked enemy aircraft in its breakaway to starboard.

'Enemy aircraft did not open fire during the fifth attack. It was last seen diving down to starboard with its port engine on fire and a flash was seen through the clouds a little later. During the attack the pilot was corkscrewing and turning to port alternatively.

'Monica gave first warning. IFF on. No flak or searchlights. Halifax was damaged along the fuselage and the rear turret also in wing, dinghy being u/s as a result. Whole action took place with one of the engines of the Halifax u/s, having been shot up over target.

Enemy aircraft claimed as "destroyed". Rounds fired: 2,000.'

Sam Liggett, the pilot continues:

'After this Me110 attack Jock informed me that the oxygen tubes had been broken and were burning; also the W/T set was smashed. Then Jock, Bill and Len set to work with fire extinguishers and anything else available to put the fire out. Desperately they worked on the fire, and after a while managed to put it out.

'Meanwhile, on checking with the rest of the crew, Lofty informed me that he was unable to move the turret or even open the doors. This was worrying, and so ordered Ginger into the Astro dome and Tich to help extricate Lofty from the tail turret. This was achieved by hacking the doors off with crash axe and hauling Lofty up to the rest bay – this was no small feat as Lofty was 6'1 (He bent his knees when he was measured, as 6' was the absolute maximum height for a gunner. Tich was 5'2.)

'Thinking that this was some sort of trip, and now hoping that nothing else would happen and that we could have a quiet time for the rest of the journey, when Ginge suddenly informed me that a Focker Wulf 190 was approaching, and this was just what I didn't want as we had no defence. I threw the aircraft into a steep port spiral and was then unable to recover. Down and down we went, and it wasn't until about 4,000 or 5,000ft that I was able to straighten up, and then I was able to use excess air speed to return us to about 10,000ft.

'The crew had been badly thrown about, and on checking with each crew member I found that fortunately only Lofty had been hurt. He had been thrown across the aircraft and sustained a very badly bruised leg. He made light of his injury.

'All the crewmembers gradually sorted themselves out after this rather grim experience. Tich returned to mid upper turret and Ginger to his position. Just then the inner starboard engine made some noises, spluttered and died. Feathered it. After all we had gone through, now was the time when I thought that we could do with some good news and as if by magic, Bill reported seeing the French coast below. It was just the thing to cheer us up.

Ginge then pulled the mat from us by advising that all tanks (12 of them) were fluttering on empty. All of a sudden, we found that we had one sort of major problem, lack of fuel, and the English Channel still to cross. Soon after and almost in unison both Bill and Tich stated that they were sure that they could see the coast ahead. At this stage we didn't know where we were, as all the maps had been destroyed in the fire.

'I made a "Darky call" [via emergency radio system] and I heard a female voice reply but couldn't understand what she said as it was totally unreadable. I took a chance and called again, advising that I was going to have to ditch the aircraft in the sea, but I was hoping to ditch close to the coast, which by this time could easily be seen as dawn was breaking.

'All the crew knew that this was going to be a very testing time, and I am sure they all had a case of nerves at this time. I didn't have time for any thoughts like that. I was desperately peering out into the semi-darkness, trying to get some sort of bearing. I was then flying at about 1,500ft and gradually losing height. I ordered all crew members into their ditching positions, and at the same time turned what was thought to be into wind. I couldn't believe my luck as just at that time the port outer engine gave up the ghost and at this time I didn't bother to feather it.

'We came down and made a good landing on the water. We were rather lucky that the sea wasn't rough. We were in some sort of bay. We actually ditched at 0450 hours on the 10th. July 1943. I ordered everyone out and the crew quickly got out and onto the port wing. We were all safe and no one had got hurt. We then had another piece of bad news, when Len informed me that the aircraft dingy was useless, as the German fighter had ripped it to shreds during the attack.

'I think from memory that we were about 150 to 200 yards off shore. Jock and Tich decided to swim for the beach. While watching them commence their swim, Lofty slipped off the wing into the sea, although he seemed to drift out to sea, it was the aircraft gradually moving closer to the coastline that gave that impression. At this time we were all wearing our Mae Wests, which we had inflated. About this time we heard an aircraft engine, and Ginge fired off the Very pistol. A Walrus aircraft appeared and circled and I saw the pilot wave. (In 1994, I was invited to the Air Sea Rescue reunion at Lyme Regis and met Tom Fletcher, the Walrus pilot) There seemed to be so much happening at once. I then saw a rescue launch approaching, and I was able to alert the launch and they picked up Lofty, none the worse for his experience. Before the launch got close enough to pick up the remainder of the crew, Len, Bill, Ginge and myself, I heard the belly of our aircraft . . . touching the gravel on the shore. That was a wonderful sound; in fact I can still hear it now. So we then waved the launch away and stepped ashore, getting just our feet wet.

'On landing from the launch, Lofty was taken to hospital and, after being examined, was found to have no serious injuries. He was discharged after 48 hours. Both Tich and Jock got to the shore safely, and as soon as the rest of us got to the shore we were met by an elderly lady in her nightclothes and dressing gown. She insisted that we follow her to her home. She took us straight into her front room, which was carpeted with a beautiful white carpet. Tich and Jock were already there, sitting comfortably with large beaming smiles on their faces. The lady just would not allow us to remove our flying boots. She served us with wonderful tea and biscuits, ideal for that time of the morning! I have often wondered how she ever got her carpet clean. Sadly, I never managed to get her name.

'We had been at the house for a little while, and soon it had become daylight. I wandered back to the foreshore and looked at the aircraft. I could see that it had suffered serious damage to the rear port vertical stabilizer, and then on further inspection found that the port rudder and starboard stabilizer had also been badly damaged. I then realized why I had had such difficulty in controlling the aircraft.

'Our fuel tanks were empty but in a way that was a blessing for us. This made the aircraft buoyant and so enabled us to float in on the tide. We were later taken by RAF transport to Brighton and then northwards back to our base at Breighton. We all then went on "survival leave".

'We all met up again and did a bit more flying, but not operational. Then, like a bolt from the blue, we were all split up for no reason that was given, not even the squadron commander could find out. I then went to pick another crew, but unfortunately I suffered breathing problems at altitude. I had numerous tests done and was eventually informed that I was unfit to fly above 15,000ft. I was rather lucky to be seconded to air transport auxiliary and had the job of ferrying aircraft all over the UK.'

What happened to the rest of the crew?

Len was grounded and posted to air traffic control.

Bill was badly injured after joining a new crew, whose plane crashed on local flying.

Jock was posted to 102 Squadron and reported missing, believed killed, in September 1943.

Ginge was also posted to 102 Squadron. He was shot down in September 1943 (*136*). The only survivor in his crew, he became a POW. He returned to this country after the war.

Tich failed to return from a mission to Hanover. I have no further information about him.

Lofty transferred to the Pathfinder force and was killed over the Ruhr on the 20th. December 1943. He is buried at Rheinberg, near Dusseldorf.

All were mentioned in dispatches for their efforts on the 9/10 July 1943.

Sam Liggett (right) at his home in Scotland with the author. [S. Liggett]

Sam Liggett then went on to explain the procedure of putting together a new operational bomber crew. It wasn't just a case of detailing a group of airmen as a crew. To put a good team together it needed several ingredients. For example, they all had to get on with each other: after all their lives might depend on the brotherly regard in which they held each other. The captain and pilot had the last say, but in a way it was the general feelings that manifested itself during various flying hours that they were together in the air, together with their social life.

'Before we became operational and were still getting the crew together,' Sam says, 'we were given a certain amount of time to meld as a team. We did eventually fill every position on the aircraft and were told that we could fly anywhere just so as to get to know each other. I asked the other guys for suggestions where we could go to and almost immediately the tail gunner, Keith Smith, suggested his home town. At this time I was unaware that the rest of the crew had arranged this destination between them. The excuse given was that Keith had always wanted to fly over his house.

'We set off and the crew settled down to their tasks as we flew westwards towards the city of Leek, Staffs. We approached the town and I asked if he, Keith, could see his house. He replied that we were a little too high but could we fly a little lower. I reduced height down to 400–500ft, a height I knew I shouldn't be flying.

'He then indicated the right area, suddenly saying, "There, that house next to the school". I then saw something falling from the aircraft. It was a small parcel, and it landed in the school playground. Keith had delivered his washing to his Mum.

'I was furious with the crew, and told them that I would see them all when we landed back at base. I had words with each and everyone telling them that they were not to pull any more strokes like that. I suppose, years after, it is quite funny, but not at the time.

'On entering the mess for lunch there was a telegram from Lofty's mother saying, "Parcel received, and all the best to the crew of 'O' for Orange"'

'I don't mind saying that I sweated for a couple of days, and it later transpired that a policeman, a friend of Lofty's family, had collected the parcel from the school playground and extracted a pair of socks to keep in the police station in case of any problems. I never heard anymore about the parcel and so was able to breathe a big sigh of relief.'

Eric Gosling's Luck

Eric ('Ginge') Gosling
[S. Liggett]

We met Sgt. Ginge Gosling in the previous story, but he was to have another narrow escape in February 1944. He was posted to no. 102 Squadron, based at Pocklington. His pilot was Flt. Lt. Tony Hilton. It was a very good crew, a group of young men pulling together.

Their first few operations consisted of what Bomber Command called 'gardening' – that is, dropping mines in selected areas of the sea. He recalls that on one occasion this was just off Norway, on another close to the Friesland Islands. These trips were mundane and uneventful. A couple of sorties to Berlin followed, these a little more exciting and at times rather frightening. Then came the fateful third trip to the German capital .

It was the 15th February 1944 when the crews received their briefing for what was to be one of the largest raids to date. It involved a number of Halifax and Lancaster bombers from several squadrons. With German forces on the run, this would be yet another nail in Hitler's coffin.

At 17.15 hours the briefing was over and it was time for these great aircraft to roll down the runway for take-off. Halifax II bomber no. LW339 DY-F-'F' for Freddie was soon airborne and heading for the rendezvous prior to the flight to Berlin. The route to be taken was across the North Sea and Denmark, turning towards the Baltic and then across to Berlin. The flight to the German border was in the main uneventful, although all members kept a wary eye for any German fighters. It was about 20.30 hours as they reached the German border. They were flying on strongly, in formation, and spot on course when without any warning the aircraft just blew up. The reason has never been fully explained but could have been a German fighter underneath and firing upwards, a favourite tactic at that time.

Eric Gosling takes up the story: 'The next thing I knew was floating down to earth by parachute. I don't remember either clipping it on, baling out or pulling the ripcord. There were scores of bits of what had been molten metal embedded in my battledress trousers and flying boots. I must have been knocked unconscious when the aircraft went up; it all seemed like a very bad dream.'

He found himself lying by the side of a roadway with part of his parachute caught in some small trees. He was the only survivor. (The rest of his crew were buried in the Berlin 1939–1945 war cemetery.) He was soon discovered by the German police and escorted, still dazed, to the local police station before being handed over to the Luftwaffe. He discovered that he was near the German town of Rostock. He spent several hours under interrogation and was then given the POW number 1471. Transported by cattle truck for 400 miles to Stalag Luft VI, he was later moved to another camp because of the Russian advance. While there he developed appendicitis, later complicated by peritonitis. A Yugoslav POW, Dr. Dusan Obradovic, who later signed his name in Eric's diary, operated on him and saved his life.

His liberation came at 8.50pm on 16th April 1945 when the British 7th Armoured Division arrived: most of the German guards had left a few days earlier. He returned to England on a stretcher and was taken to the hospital at RAF Cosford where it took six months for him to recover. He left the RAF as a warrant officer and returned to his trade as a butcher. He opened his own shop in Broad Street, Stafford, in 1946 and remained there for the next 20 years.

He is very proud of the fact that he is a member of both the Goldfish and the Caterpillar clubs,and feels that he was very lucky to survive the war.

Later records indicate that the Halifax bomber was hit by flak and that the remains of the aircraft crashed at Bartelshagen, Germany. Another of the no. 102 Squadron Halifax bombers was also shot down around the same time. All the crew were killed, and they are buried in the same cemetery.

Theodore Rhodes' Story

It was early morning and the American B17 crews at Snetterton Heath, Norfolk, were assembled for briefing. There was the usual rather nervous chatter, each of them asking himself the same question: 'Will it be Germany again today?'

The senior officer arrived flanked by two subordinates who made their way onto the low stage at the end of the room. He talked about the previous raid, adding encouraging words for the forthcoming one. He spoke at length about the war effort and the American involvement. He then uncovered the wall charts. Yes, the 'target for today' was Durin – Germany again.

A short while later the crews began making their way out of the building and towards their aircraft. Once again, private thoughts took over, their minds wandering over many subjects, ranging from their college days, their families right through to the mission of today. Would they be coming back? These young men, though full of spirit, were very aware of the dangers they would soon be facing.

Theodore 'Dusty' Rhodes in early 1943. [T. Rhodes]

At 6.20am precisely on Wednesday 20th. October 1943, on a dark and very dismal morning, the airfield at Snetterton Heath was suddenly turned into full-blown life – a sight worth seeing as the engines began to roar and these massive aircraft began trundling into their positions. A good run, and one by one they took to the air, a wonderful pageant to behold.

This is the story of just one of those B17s and one member of its crew, Temporary Sergeant Theodore 'Dusty' Rhodes, service no. 14124590 We join it on take-off – Flying Fortress no. 42-37749, taxiing into position, its pilot, 2nd. Lt. William Spence Jones, all the while carefully watching the aircraft in front of him. With a massive roar of its four engines, the aircraft was quickly airborne, its bomb load secure. Very soon it had made the correct height for joining the formation which, its course selected, was headed for Germany.

The crew is as follows:

2nd Lt. William Jones	(pilot)
2nd Lt. Karl Bliss jn.	(co-pilot)
2nd Lt. William Neiderkorn	(navigator)
2nd Lt. Raymond Gillam	(bombardier)
T/Sgt. Theodore Rhodes	(top turret gunner)
T/Sgt. John Pollock	(radio operator)
T/Sgt. Earl Hebbard	(left waist gunner)
T/Sgt. Julius Kaufman	(right waist gunner)
T/Sgt. Thomas Griffie	(tail gunner)
T/Sgt. Leland Welch	(ball turret gunner)

It was a pretty uneventful flight over to Germany, Theodore Rhodes, the top gunner, later reported. They had their fair share of flak, but no German fighters attacked them.

'I think it was somewhere about three hours before we reached the target. Although it was a cloudy and wet day, the target was soon identified. The bombs doors opened slowly and deliberately, and one by one the bombs left our aircraft on their way down. I think we were all relieved when the doors were closed, the pilot, over the radio, confirmed the doors being closed. We then banked to port and started on the long journey home.

'However, what had been a fairly good journey out quickly changed to becoming a very rough mission. The flak was very heavy and their aim was good. This, together with a large number of German fighters suddenly appearing, made for a pretty frightening experience. All the gunners were kept very busy. I suppose we were lucky, as many of our colleagues were being shot down. We watched horrified, as one by one our colleagues and friends failed to bale out and crashed to their deaths. All the aircraft in our vicinity were getting peppered with the heavy flak.

'With the bombs gone the aircraft was much lighter. We were flying at 31,000ft and trying to get above the heavy flak, but due to the bad weather we were in the clouds for almost the entire flight home. The navigator, Bill Neiderkorn, had set a course of 270°, and we were flying blind following this course. The pilot was having a lot of trouble controlling the aircraft, as one by one the engines were packing up. Just by virtue of the time we had been flying on the homeward course, it was judged that we must be over the Channel, although at this time we couldn't see it.

'About this time three of our four engines had gone and the 4th one started to play up. We all realized that the aircraft was in trouble, although no one said anything. As well as losing the engines we had lost our electricity. We were also losing height, fast.

'All of a sudden we came out of the clouds and we could see land and as we did so the fourth engine started to splutter, things weren't good. By this time we were down to little more than 4,000ft but the worst thing of all, we didn't know where we were. We were still losing height and pilot Jones said we should ditch the aircraft but didn't have enough control of the plane, and so we decided that the only option left to us was to bale out. No electricity, three engines gone, the fourth almost, and then to add to this we were still losing altitude fast – an exciting position for us! The pilot had made his decision and shouted, "Hit the Silk!"

'We called out "Hit the Silk!" as we baled out, so that everyone knew what was happening. I was lucky as I used an emergency chute which is very small – some say it was an 18ft chute. I was the top turret gunner and couldn't use the usual back or bucket chute. I recall that I jumped into a strong 40mph ground wind and was very pleased when I felt and saw my parachute open.

'I drifted down, watching all the time what was below me. I got lower and was then starting to get perturbed. As I approached the ground I saw a farmhouse with smoke coming from the chimney. I knew I had to miss this and adjusted my chute accordingly. With the wind at my back I hit the ground running, luckily without any injuries. I started to gather up my parachute and, looking around, I couldn't see any of my crew. Just then a farmwoman approached me and stuck a pitchfork within a few inches of my face, just as a farmer came up with a gun, holding me prisoner. I gave them my rank and serial number and I heard them mumbling and then recognised English sounds. I quickly acted, saying "American" and they smiled. That was a relief.

'I opened my flight suit and offered chewing gum. I found out later that they were members of the local home guard, and were expecting an invasion by the Germans. Many more members of the home guard came and offered to help me find the other members of my crew.

'We eventually all met up, but some of the crew had been hurt. John Pollack, the radio operator was seriously injured with a broken back. The co-pilot, Karl Bliss jnr., suffered a broken arm and the ball turret gunner, Leland Welch, had a bad head injury, sustained when he struck some farm machinery. Various other crewmembers had bruises and cuts.

'I later found out that we landed at a small village called Southease, Sussex, between a farm and the eastern side of a small

---

FLYING FORTRESS NO. 42-37749

Crashed at Beddingham Hill, near Furlongs Farm, Lewes, East Sussex, Wednesday 20th October 1943. These details, although sketchy and in note form, are taken from the county controller's journal. They come from different sources.

From Lewes: 13.40 hours – Flying Fortress has crashed in flames at Beddingham.

From Seaford: 13.40 hours – Large bomber crashed approximately 3 miles north of Seaford.

From Newhaven: 13.45 hours – Fortress crashed behind Tarring Neville. Crew baled out near Southease.

From Chailey: 13.50 hours – Fortress crashed on Beddingham Hill, 2 men baled out. Plane burning. NFS attending from Lewes and Newhaven.

From Lewes: 13.53 hours – Ambulance sent at 13.51 hours to Iford.

From Newhaven: 13.55 hours – Fortress seen to crash and one man bale out 5 miles north east of Newhaven.

From Newhaven: 14.42 hours – Crew of plane taken away by ambulance.

From Chailey: 14.55 hours – 9 of the Fortress crew accounted for.

From Newhaven: 16.35 hours – All crew accounted for, plane crashed at map reference 888256. Incident timed at 13.37 hours.

---

river. [The Ouse.] After we landed, we were taken to a British fighter base, where all the crew was accounted for. We were taken back to Snetterton Heath, where we were able to relax.

'This was my sixth mission and by far the worst, quite an experience. I didn't know at the time, but there was to be quite a lot more excitement in the coming months, before I made it back to the States.

'The next morning, I was told to report to the Flight Line for flying. The Air Force policy was to fly again as soon as possible after a crash in order to avoid time for you to think about it. However, my next mission was on the 3rd November, when the target was Wilhelmshaven, Holland, with a take off time at 6.35am.'

The 'excitement' that Theodore Rhodes referred to included the following incidents recorded by him while serving with the 337 Squadron, 96 Bomb Group of the 3rd.Division 8th. USAAF, 45 Combat Wing.

'I was in a mid-air crash with a Mosquito bomber on 5th. February 1944. Our B17 landed on one wheel and ground looped. The British bomber came up from 4 o'clock low and took out our no. 3 and no. 4 engines, as well as damaging the no. 2 propeller and landing gear. The pilot, ordered me, the engineer gunner, to check out the damage, which was no. 2 and 3 engines out and one right landing gear damaged. The controls were not damaged, so I reported flyable and I proceeded to crank the left wheel down. The excellent pilot flew left wing low and we landed and walked away. A near miss is a good miss. After cranking down the left landing gear, we landed on one wheel and ground-looped – another thrilling experience.'

The Mosquito concerned, no. DZ548 GB-J, of 105 Squadron, was on a training flight. The crew, Flt.Lt. J. Slatter and FO P. Hedges had taken off from Marham. The Mosquito crashed at Colne Field Farm, near St. Ives, Huntingdonshire. Both airmen were killed.

A further story reports that a B17, piloted by Captain Thomas, was on a practice flight, in a three-plane formation approximately three miles north-west of Ely, Cambridgeshire, when a British Mosquito rose up from the clouds and hit the underside of the B17. The no. 2 propeller cut into the trailing edge of the Mosquito's wing and cut it in half. The navigator in the B17 stated that both of the Mosquito crewmembers seemed to be staring down, unaware of their impending doom. Although the B17 suffered damage, Capt. Thomas brought his crew safely down.

Theodore recalls an incident on another mission:

'I remember a bomber up above us on the "bomb run" releasing its bombs . . . One of the bombs went between the nacelle of no. 3 engine and the fuselage of our plane.

'One of the hardest things to adjust to when flying in fog was to be able to see the wing tip lights, as you climb to get above the clouds and join in the assembly of planes. In our training at Walla Walla, Washington or maybe Mose Lake, we had a sudden loss of control of our plane. I was thrown to the top of the plane and finally got on my

---

SNETTERTON HEATH

Snetterton Heath air base was situated on the southern side of the A11 main road, six miles south-west of Attleborough, Norfolk.

The airfield was constructed in 1942 at a cost of £950,000. The main runway was 2,000 yards in length, with the auxiliary runways being 1,400 yards each. Originally 36 hard standings were constructed as the base was intended for use by the RAF. When it was rescheduled for use by the USAAF another 14 hard standings were constructed, making 50 in all.

The total area of concrete laid was 530,000 square yards, as well as storage being provided for a total of 144,000 gallons of fuel.

The first 8th Air Force group to arrive at Snetterton Heath were the 386th Bomb Group with B26 aircraft in June 1943, but they stayed for only one week, being transferred to north Essex to join other B26 units.

These were replaced in the middle of June by the 96th Bomb Group with B17F Flying Fortresses. Although they were already operational, they went on to fly more than 300 missions from this base.

As the most conveniently reached station from 3rd Division Headquarters at Elveden Hall, Snetterton Heath units often led major operations carrying commanding generals. General Curtis LeMay led the famous Regensburg shuttle mission to North Africa flying out of this base. The 96th also led the 3rd Division on the famous Schweinfurt mission of the 14th October 1943.

A memorial window to the 96th Bomb Group can be seen in the church at Quidenham.

The airfield fell into disuse after the war, and in 1952 it was privately purchased with a view to using the concrete runways and perimeter tracks for road racing. This proved to be a successful enterprise.

feet after the downdraft caused us to drop at least 5,000ft. I remember pilot Jones and co-pilot Bliss pulling with all their strength to pull the controls back in order to control the plane as we had a close call.

'Coming back from my 18th or 19th mission we were shot up and the oxygen system in the back of the plane was out. This meant that coming out of high altitude the lack of oxygen made you pass out or act differently. Heroic efforts by the waist gunner, Jules Kaufman, and ball turret gunner, Leland Welch, were able to pull the tail gunner, Tommie Griffin, out of the tail gun area. They did not unload the two 50-calibre guns. After I shot flares for landing and checked the tail wheel to see if it was down, we were in the process of landing when the tail wheel went back up. Our plane went crazy all over the runway and the twin 50s shot up the area, causing many investigations. I was able however, to convince the authorities that the tail wheel was down and that the electrical system was damaged from flak or bullets.

'Another time we were shot up and running out of gas. Our pilot asked me to transfer gas from nos. 2 and 3 tanks to nos. 1 and 4 engines, so that we could fly a little longer. We were really in trouble as we came into England flying between the cables that were everywhere to confuse the Germans. We landed at a British base and were refuelled and returned to our own base.

'On more than one occasion I was told by pilot Jones to get the bombs loose that were stuck in the bomb-bay. All I had was a screwdriver, so I walked through the catwalk without my emergency chute and held on to the catwalk with my left arm and used the screwdriver to shake or cause the shackle to release the two bombs that were stuck. I didn't have time to realise that the bomb-bay doors were open and that flak was everywhere. Later I said, "I must be nuts".

'A similar story, on a different mission: pilot Jones told me that there were two or three bombs still stuck in their shackles. This time I asked the radio operator to hold on to me, as I couldn't get the shackle to release. So I straddled the open bomb-bay door and put my foot on the right pad and shook the bottom bomb and caused it to fall. Then the next one fell. I crawled back through the catwalk and gave two thumbs up. I was exhausted but pilot Jones was happy and said to get those guns going – what a life!

'On one mission two of our enlisted men "borrowed" several cases of 50-calibre ammunition from a bomber who was not going on a mission at the last minute. These two gunners loaded the extra ammunition in the plane. Our pilot cornered me, the engineer, about having a hard time taking off as we were almost near the trees before we got up. I mentioned this to the crew and they asked me if I remembered running out of ammunition. I said, "Yes, I remember," so they confessed that they had overloaded the plane – but we didn't run out of ammunition.'

As in the film Memphis Belle (the story of the first 25th mission by a B17 crew), it was true that as each aircrew member completed 25 missions he would be sent home to the USA and out of the European war. T/Sgt. Theodore Rhodes, service serial no. 14124590, was one of them. Here is a complete list of his missions:

1	06.40hrs	2nd October 1943	Emden
2	07.00hrs	4th October 1943	Frankfurt
3	06.30hrs	8th October 1943	Bremen
4	05.45hrs	10th October 1943	Munster
5	08.30hrs	14th October 1943	Schweinfurt
6	06.20hrs	20th October 1943	Durin
7	06.35hrs	3rd November 1943	Wilhelmshaven
8	07.10hrs	5th November 1943	Gelsenkiriken
9	08.00hrs	10th November 1943	Gelsenkiriken
10	07.30hrs	29th November 1943	Bremen
11	06.45hrs	11th December 1943	Emden
12	08.50hrs	13th December 1943	Keil
13	07.15hrs	20th December 1943	Bremen
14	06.00hrs	22nd December 1943	Munster
15	05.30hrs	24th December 1943	France
16	08.10hrs	30th December 1943	Ludwigshafen
17	07.00hrs	31st December 1943	Paris
18	08.30hrs	5th January 1944	Bordeaux
19	07.00hrs	7th January 1944	Ludwigshafen
20	05.30hrs	21st January 1944	France
21	05.15hrs	24th January 1944	Frankfurt
22	07.15hrs	29th January 1944	Frankfurt
23	06.25hrs	3rd February 1944	Wilhelmshaven
24	06.30hrs	4th February 1944	Frankfurt
25	07.45hrs	10th February 1944	Praunschweig

All but the last of these missions was piloted by William Spence Jones.

'The pilot for the last mission was Captain Norman Thomas, known as a hot pilot with many hours experience flying B26s or A20s. He was the same pilot who had the crash with the Mosquito and got us down safely. The reason for the change of pilot was that 2nd. Lt. William Jones, our regular pilot had completed his 25 missions one before us. We were able to choose our pilot for the last and 25th mission. We chose Norman Thomas, as we firmly believed that he would get us home.

'About a month after flying our 25th.mission, on the 8th. March 1944, Captain Thomas was shot down by enemy fighters and became a POW. A month later, 8th. April 1944, T/Sgt. Leland Welch's aircraft crashed near Polder, Holland and he became a POW.'

Lastly, after the 25th. mission, and when he returned to the States, Theodore went to Miami Beach to be evaluated. He was notified that he had been in extremely hazardous combat and was assigned to non-flying duty at Gore Field in Great Falls, Montana. He had obtained a B.S. degree from Clemson University.

After the war he attended Auburn Veterinary School in Auburn, Alabama, receiving a Doctor of Veterinary degree in June 1949 and practised medicine for 37 years in North Charleston, South Carolina. He retired in 1986.

He told me that his children had difficulty in believing his wartime stories and experiences. Having read this, can you blame them?

The Tale of Winsome Winn II

This story of B17 Flying Fortress no. 42–37793 SO–X begins during the early hours of the morning of Tuesday 8th February 1944, at Grafton Underwood, a USAAF base in Northamptonshire. The airfield was home to the 305th and 384th Bomb Group, both being part of the 1st Bomb Division 8th USAAF.

The crews were briefed and very soon the bomb group division was dispatching 120 aircraft, their engines roaring. The target this morning was the marshalling yards at Frankfurt.

'Spirit of Winsome Winn 11' and her crew. Standing, left to right: Norman DeFrees (pilot), Ivan Moody (navigator), Ellis Miller (bombardier), George Hunt (co-pilot). Kneeling, left to right: Lloyd Moore (top turret gunner), Luther E. Smith (ball turret gunner), John 'Hap' Ecker (right waist gunner), Jack Kushner (tail gunner), Harley Hallam (left waist gunner) William Wright (radio operator).

One of the B17s that took off this dark morning was named 'Spirit of Winsome Winn II', and it was being flown by 2nd Lt. Norman DeFrees, with nine other crew members. They had been together for quite a while and had already been involvd in one drama little more than a month earlier when, flying a different aircraft, they were forced to crash-land at Little Staunton, another American base, due to undercarriage failure. That aircraft was a write-off, but luckily the crew, athough shaken, were unharmed.

On another flight, a practice mission, and with another crew's aircraft, there had yet again been a problem with the landing gear. This time Norman DeFrees bellied the aircraft in to make a perfect landing, his marvellous flying skills ensuring that none of the crew suffered any injuries.

Norman DeFrees vividly recalls the 8th of February:

'It was a rare and beautiful day over western Europe, and very clear. We had assembled after take-off at 28,000 feet, having a very strong westerly wind, and arrived without incident. The flight took around two hours. We were over the target and released our bombs. I remember that it was so clear that you could actually see the snow on the ground and the muzzle flash of the German anti-aircraft 88 guns on the ground. It was at this point, just after "bombs away", that a huge blast of black flak appeared above the nose, a short distance ahead of the aircraft. I noted the oil pressure start to fall on the left outboard engine and I quickly hit the "feather" button. A few seconds later I noticed the same thing occurring to the right outboard, and got it feathered too.

'Our nose dropped, and despite full throttle and 45in of manifold pressure on the two inboard engines, we were losing height at approximately 150ft per minute and only able to fly at 95mph.

'I called for the navigator, Ivan Moody, and was informed that he would be along shortly. When he did arrive I told him the problems that we had and that we needed a different course to get home. He plotted a great course and we evaded any further flak.

'I called the radio room and told Wright, the radio operator, to get Smitty (Luther Smith), the ball turret gunner, out of there and to see if between them they could drop the ball turret in order to lessen the weight of the plane. At this point, about the French border, we were down from 28,000ft to only 8,000ft. I felt the ball turret go and the plane's speed immediately leapt from 95mph to 110mph – not a lot but very reassurring – and it was then that I decided to let the aircraft down to 1,500ft, this then giving relief to the two inboard engines, which had by then been operating at full take-off power for more than three and a half hours. This was quite remarkable, as they should only operate at full power for about five minutes.

'We kept on course for England, and it wasn't long before the English Channel was in sight. I knew we were still not out of trouble, telling the crew to prepare for ditching in the Channel. I then called Air Sea Rescue.

'We met two Spitfires about mid-Channel, and one of them did a vertical bank directly in front of our plane, which I took to mean, "Follow me". We cleared the Channel, coming in over England at about 500ft above the terrain.

'I then thought I saw an airfield. I lowered the landing gear and put the plane into a bank, preparing to land. Just then red flares shot up from the field, and I saw tanks beginning to move around on what I had taken to be an airfield.

'The Spitfire again signalled to me to follow and we then headed across to Brighton. While we were flying over the town, the right inboard motor ran out of gas.

'Now, we had a bit more of a problem, and I needed to get down as soon as possible. From my perspective there appeared to be less habitation to my right. As I put the nose down, the navigator shouted, "Get over the wires!" I said, "crash-landing." Ivan, the navigator, came running up from the nose to the radio room and this was the first realisation that he had been hit. (He had been injured by flak while we were over the target in Germany.) His head was swathed in gauze.

'As I looked down at the terrain, I saw the 120,000-volt power lines and a ditch of some thirty yards in width, and a ploughed hillside ascending directly away from the ditch. The right wing of our plane was heading for the metal tower supporting the power lines, and at the same time I realised that I was so close to the ground that if I attempted to bank, my left wing tip would go into the ground. I yelled at George Hunt, my co-pilot, "Follow me through!" There was no time for dithering. We both turned right aleron into the tower and both stepped full on the rudder. The plane did a nice "flat crab" to the left. The plane hit on the landing gear on this side of the ditch and ballooned across the ditch under the wires and ballooned again up the ploughed hillside. We then just pulled the stick back and plopped into the muck.

'Our speed on landing was about 70mph, and the time we landed was somewhere between 12 noon and 1 pm, I can't remember exactly. I know that if our landing gear had not been down, we would have gone nose down first into that ditch.'

Luther Smith, the aircraft's ball turret' gunner, has his own version of the story:

'We had a very strong west wind that day, and in a short while we were over the target. Flak knocked out two of our engines while we were still over the target. I am not sure which ones were hit but I think the inboard ones, nos. 2 and 3. At the same time our navigator, Ivan Moody, from Kansas, was hit. A piece of flak went through his steel infantry helmet that he was wearing on top of his leather flying helmet. The flak creased the top of his head. The bombardier, Ellis Miller from Illinois, put a bandage on Moody and then went back to work on his blood-stained charts. Flying on only two engines, we

A rare photograph of Winsome Winn 11 after crash-landing at Patcham, near Brighton. Norman DeFrees has verified the picture as authentic.

could not stay with the rest of the formation, and the wind that had helped us make a quick trip to the target was now something we could have done without. At one time, Moody estimated that our ground speed was only about 60mph.

'We dumped the ball turret somewhere over France and until then we were losing altitude so badly that we would not have made it, even to the Channel. The turret weighed 1,290 pounds, then the weight of the ammunition, and getting rid of it jumped our airspeed up by something like 20mph and this in turn, slowed our descent.

'As far as I can tell, we were the first crew to jettison the ball turret actually on a mission. Throughout the remainder of the war, several crews dropped their ball turrets. The only thing we should have done was to have kept the ball turretgun sight, as apparently they were in short supply and very expensive.

'Crossing the Channel, we prepared for ditching in the sea. None of us thought our gas supply would last.

'Spitfires met us over the Channel and were escorting us to a grass fighter field near to Brighton [the airfield was at Shoreham] when, on approach with our wheels down, the third engine quit. Our pilot, 2nd Lt. Norman DeFrees, saw a patch of ploughed ground and made for it. The navigator, Ivan Moody, suddenly saw wires in the split seconds that were left to make a decision,

'DeFrees knew that he couldn't get over the wire, with just power from one engine so decided to make a crash-landing under them. (These cables were carrying 120,000 volts) It was a good job of flying, and we were all so proud of the two men in the pilots' seats.

'With the two emergency-type landings which our pilot Norman had made, there was complete faith in our pilots, knowing that they would do everything possible to bring us home safely – after all, it was their butts as well as ours. Even so, the welfare of the crew was uppermost in their minds.

'Just a word about the cold at high altitudes. It certainly was very cold: everyone wore electrically heated suits, with the waist gunners also wearing fleece lined suits.

'Incidently, not only had our pilot proved his immaculate skill, but when we were on the approach to the field, the engine quit. Then not only did Norman have to set the plane down immediately,

PILOT'S SKILL SAVED HIS CREW

ADVENTURES OF A FLYING FORTRESS

A N American Flying Fortress pilot saved his machine and crew from certain destruction on Tuesday, when he flew beneath high tension cables to bring off an amazing two-engine landing near a South of England

"Late Christopher Bean"

PLAY PRESENTED AT BRIGHTON

The Withdean Players gave their third public performance of the well-known mystery comedy, "The Late Christopher

Evidence of the splendid workmanship put into the Fortress, and the skill and courage of its pilot, was outstanding. The Fortress had been mauled by flak. Two of its engines were not functioning, while two members of the crew had been hit, one in the wrist, the other in the head, but neither wounds were of a serious character.

Over the Channel the plane lost height and the pilot considered a forced landing near the coast but decided to

A report of the incident in the Brighton & Hove Gazette, 12th February 1944.

going under the high tension cables, but he also had to side slip to avoid hitting the tower, where the cables were affixed, with the wing tip.'

There was, Norman DeFrees says, just one minor injury: 'We all exited the aircraft and gathered around one of the crew, who had sprained his ankle on jumping to the ground from the radio room hatch, which is quite high when the aircraft is standing on its landing gear. I was later told that my co-pilot George Hunt may have said a prayer. The gathering around the airman who sprained his ankle may have been mistaken for group prayer.

'I believe that a postman was the first on the scene and then, not long after the landing, the local police from Brighton arrived. We were flown back to our base at Grafton Underwood on a B17 out of Shoreham on the 10th February.'

Luther Smith has a happy memory of this time: 'After we were down a while, a gentleman climbed the hill to where we were with a huge picnic basket filled with sandwiches, two large thermos bottles of tea and a bottle of cognac. I will never forget his greeting – "I say, Yanks, that was a jolly good landing." It was nice of him to have done this for us, as I do believe that the tea laced with cognac was the best I ever tasted.'

The 'gentleman' who took the picnic basket to the crew was Robert Swan, who together with his wife Maud owned and ran the Belmont boarding kennels (now the RSPCA kennels on the main London Road at Patcham). He actually was the first person to reach the plane.

Following the crash-landing, members of the RAF regiment based at Shoreham arrived to guard the aircraft. A day or so later a team of engineers from the 8th Air Force base began to carry out the repairs, which took several days. The ground was prepared, hedges were cut down and ditches were filled in readiness for take-off. When the repair work was completed, the people living in the Church Hill area of Patcham were temporally evacuated from their homes as a precaution. The Flying Fortress, opening up each engine in turn, and with the smallest crew possible, turned to face southwards and then, with a great roar, took off and was flown back to its base at Grafton Underwood.

On the return to their base, the Winsome Winn II crew were assigned to a brand new B17-G Fortress, still in its bright silver paint, – no camouflaging. The crew, with Norman DeFrees as pilot, took off on the morning of 22nd February 1944 – just 14 days after their crash-landing incident at Patcham, Brighton. Their mission, on this day, was to bomb Aschersleben in Germany. This B17 had no name but its Registration number was S/N 42-97488 SO – (544 Squadron).

Norman DeFrees recalls: 'Together with a large number of other planes we were given the target of Ascherleben, Germany, taking off at 4am. England had clouds up to 28,000 feet, and the assembly was a mess. Our group ran through another group at right angles, and by the time it was over each group had lost one plane and crew. To add to our problems, the fighter escort couldn't get off.

'The German fighters met us in mid-Channel and our plane was the deputy lead, high squadron on the right. The formation was a new, unworkable concept. We had always flown wings in trail. On this day it was supposed to be wings abreast. Someone overlooked the fact that if the lead flew at an airspeed of 150mph the planes on the outside of a turn would have to fly 220–250mph to maintain formation. This was the one and only time this was attempted.

'After about an hour of Me109 fighter attacks, during which we would take small-jinks evasive action as the tail gunner would elate the direction on incoming fighter attacks, I went to dump the nose a slight amount and the plane went into a vertical dive of 9,000ft. The co-pilot and I finally got the plane under control.

'We had released our bombs and turned back towards England. We planned to make gradual let-down to the deck, but needless to say our faith in the stability of the aircraft was badly shaken. I asked the tail gunner what had happened to our plane, and he replied that most of the horizontal empinage was shot away. The right inboard motor was shot out, windmilling and causing vibration. He then shouted, "Look over your shoulder!" and I saw 12–15 Me109s coming up beneath us, and I gave the order to bale out. We were at 13,000ft. I got up and looked down at the nose: the navigator and bombardier were out.

'I went back through the bomb bay – the doors were open; all the crewmen had baled out. All this time I am walking around with my legstraps to my backpack parachute dangling around my ankles. I jumped out of the bomb bay and did a free fall for approximately 5,000ft and then pulled the 'D' ring. I felt the shock of my weight against my underarms and was, thankfully, able to hold on till touch-down. The only ill effects from my stupidity were two huge bruises under each armpit.

'A village constable took me in tow to a crossroad, where the rest of the crew, except Ivan Moody the navigator, was. He had already been taken to hospital with serious wounds. Smitty was lying on the ground, with his right hand and his arm halfway to his elbow severed. He asked for a cigarette, and I lit one for him and stuck it in his mouth. The co-pilot, George Hunt, bombardier Ellis Miller and myself, went to Stalag Luft 1 at Barth, Germany and we were returned to the USA in May 1945.'

The aircraft crashed near Wesel in Germany, bursting into flames. Luther Smith had suffered the serious injuries to his right arm during the attack and had therefore been unable to put his parachute on. Realising his predicament, another crew member quickly strapped on a spare one, affixing it to the 'static' line and pushing him out. 'Smitty' was taken to hospital, where his right arm was amputated. Some eight months after being shot down he was released through the Red Cross and returned to the USA.

As for Winsome Winn II, on 11th March 1944, after being fully repaired, she was returned to the 384th Bomb Group and taken over by a new crew who had recently completed their training and had just flown in from the USA.

Just a week later, piloted by Lt. Roger E. Smith, she took off on a bombing mission to Oberffenhofen in Germany. The aircraft was shot down, crash-landing in Switzerland, where the crew were interned. The damaged aircraft was eventually dismantled and taken by train to Dabendorf.

WINSOME WINN AT PATCHAM – SOME EYE-WITNESS ACCOUNTS

Trevor Evans, retired Brighton fireman stated that during the afternoon of Tuesday 8th February 1944, he was a young lad and standing in the playground of his school in Patcham. A huge American bomber flew very low over the school and made a forced landing on the Downs behind Court Farm.

He recalls:'I ran from my school, all the way up to the farm and when I got there, I was given a lift by a friendly Land Army girl on her tractor. We went up to the grounded aircraft. On arrival, I was amazed to see the crew, some sitting and some laying on the grass near to their downed aircraft."

Bob Trulove says: 'In February 1944, I was 13 years old. My father had seen very 'active' service with the British Expeditionary Force (BEF) in France. He was wounded before Dunkirk and was one of the last to make it back to England. He was given a small pension and invalided out of the army –– the family all back together. The regulations of the war forbade civilians to use cameras or binoculars: film was short and so the non-usage of cameras was no great deal. My mother carried a rather large handbag – among other personal items the bag also contained a large pair of brass marine field glasses.

'On February 8th 1944, the whole family were out together on the racecourse at Brighton. We had found a rather nice sheltered spot, out of the cool breeze, at the top of Wilson Avenue, close to where it crosses the race course. The weather was quite pleasant with weak sunshine. From this point we had a good view of the sea and from the activity over a period we knew that the invasion of Europe wasn't too far away.

'We noticed, while looking out to sea, very low down and far away, a smoke haze was forming. Using the field glasses, we could see, as it got a little closer, that it was an aeroplane in trouble. It was flying very low down and had been badly shot up. We identified it as a Flying Fortress and then suddenly we realised that it was flying

GRAFTON UNDERWOOD

Grafton Underwood was located in well-wooded countryside, about four miles north-east of Kettering, Northamptonshire.

It was originally planned as a bomber station for the RAF, being constructed in 1941. The runways were 1,600 yards long, and were to prove unsuitable for the heavy American bombers which were due to be based there. In 1942 the length of the main runway was increased to 2,000 yards and smaller ones of some 1,400 yards were constructed. The main runway was sited to run from north-east to south-west.

By the time the American Air Force were due to move in, a lot of work had been achieved: 50 hard standings were built as well as two T2 hangers. Eleven other sites were built, comprising communal and barrack blocks which were in the main dispersed within the countryside to the east of the base.

Grafton Underwood was the very first airfield in England to receive an 8th Air Force flying unit when on 12th May 1942 the personnel of 15th Bomb Squadron arrived to begin training on Boston light bombers for action with the RAF. The airfield at this stage was lacking in many facilities and so the unit was moved, in early June, to Molesworth.

This base is famous for launching the very first US heavy bomber raid from this country. The first raid, a bombing operation on Rouen on 17th August, was carried out by 342nd and 414th Squadrons.

On 12th September 1942 the first elements of another B-17 group arrived from the USA, the 305th commanded by Colonel Curtis LeMay. This group began operations from Grafton in the November.

The next group, was the 96th, which arrived towards the end of April 1943, beginning operations about two weeks later. This group was assigned to the 4th Wing with a general base in the northern part of Essex, and moved at the end of May.

Their place was taken by a new group new in from the States, the 384th Bomb Group, which went operational in June. This was 2nd Lieutenant Norman DeFrees' Group. This bomb group remained at Grafton for about two years, eventually moving to Istres, France after D-Day. Almost 350 bombing operations were carried out from this airfield during the war period.

The runways were removed in 1966 after the airfield reverted back to the estate of The Duke of Buccleugh.

On Sunday 25th September 1977 a memorial was unveiled at the southern end of the old main runway by William Dolan, an 81-year-old First World War fighter pilot with the American Expeditionary Force who also saw active service in the Second World War although he was over age.

almost directly towards us. At this point we became very concerned, as we were not sure if it would clear the Race Hill. We watched, awestruck, as the massive aircraft kept coming on towards where we were standing up. We watched as it came over the green tiled roofs of those houses by East Brighton Golf course, seemingly staggering through the air, flying like a wet soggy blanket.

The control tower at Grafton Underwood in August 1942, showing Maj. Gen Carl Spaatz (right, with hands in pockets) and Col. Frank Castle (foot on rail). [USAAF]

'As the plane got even nearer to us we could clearly see that smoke was coming out of one engine, the propeller rotating very, very slowly – in fact hardly at all. Another propeller had stopped altogether. The aircraft was leaving an oily smoke haze behind it, which was what had first attracted our attention when it was out over the Channel.

'There were large holes blown through the wings and the body, through which we could clearly see the daylight. One undercarriage leg was hanging down and there were many wires trailing from the aircraft. The noise was deafening, it was so low. We were still not sure that the aircraft would get over the race course hill. However, it passed over, just to our right – in fact between our position and the top of Bear Road. The Fortress was only about 50ft or possibly 75ft up and slowly made its way over towards Hollingbury. We saw it just about stagger over Hollingbury golf course and we continued to stand and stare in absolute awed amazement. What a scene we had just witnessed: this was something I would never forget.

'As we continued to look northwards it went, with our silent prayers that it would get down safely, especially after flying back all that way in such a terrible condition.'

Vic Johnson, then 10 years old, was near the top of Ditchling Road with some friends. It was dinner time, and although it was cold, it was dry and sunny: 'I heard a very loud noise coming from the sky, I looked up and saw a very large bomber, flying above us and coming in from the sea. I thought it would crash into the top of the houses as it was flying so low, it was barely above the rooftops.

There was a stream of what looked like oil or something trailing behind it and it sort of shimmered in the sunshine. The propellers were not turning and it was obvious that there was something wrong. The plane wasn't flying straight, one wing was lower than the other one. There were holes in the side of it and a big one underneath. I just knew it was going to crash. We stood and watched it; lots of people were staring up at it. They were standing on the pavement and didn't move until the plane went out of sight. It went over towards Hollingbury and Patcham.

'I lost sight of it and I expected to hear a big explosion when it crashed, but there was no such noise of an explosion. I just stood there waiting for the explosion, stood there for a long time but nothing happened. I went home wondering what could have happened.

'The next day everyone was talking about the American Flying Fortress that came down in a field at Patcham the previous afternoon. It came down just above the playing fields at Braypool, just above the kennels.'

The last words go to Luther Smith (Smitty):

'Thinking about the landing at Patcham, we had a phrase that covered our thoughts after a rough mission, 'Good old terra ferma – the more firmer, the less terror.'

Survivors from Winsom Winn, in a photograph take in 2000. Left to right: Norman DeFrees, Luther Smith (Smitty) and Jack Kushner. [N. DeFrees]

An Air Sea Rescue

At 8.30pm on 8th May 1944 an air sea rescue aircraft brought into Shoreham in Sussex three members of a downed B17 Flying Fortress, which had come down in the Channel.

Nineteen B17s had taken part in a raid on Sottevast on the Cherbourg peninsula, the target being important anti-invasion installations. They took off at 1600 hours from Grafton Underwood, their route taking them out over Portland Bill and across the enemy coast at Couville.

Throughout the entire bomb run flak was intense and very accurate. The American bombers dropped their loads at a height of 26,000ft at 1902 hours and quickly made a turn to the right, reducing height by 1,000ft but soon gaining 500ft before starting the descent. Four aircraft were lost on this mission – three over enemy territory. The fourth, no. 42–9708, was hit and badly damaged by flak as it neared Cherbourg. The pilot, James Brown, desperately juggled with the controls, but ditched in the English Channel about 15 miles from Cherbourg. The plane's position was noted by one of the other B17s in the group and radioed through to the air sea rescue units.

Only three of the 10-man crew were picked up, all suffering from shock because of the time they had spent immersed in the water. One of them, Staff Sergeant Donald Reis, the waist gunner, was found to be dead on arrival at Shoreham and was taken to the local mortuary. The two survivors, who were taken to Southlands Hospital, were Lt. W. Kube, the tail gunner, and Staff Sergeant George Yeager.

The seven other members of the crew were never found, and their names appear on 'the walls of the missing'.

Bibliography

249 at War, Brian Cull
Aces High, volumes 1 and 2, Christopher Shores and Clive Williams
Battle of Britain, Then and Now, Winston Ramsey (*ed.*)
Bomber Command Losses, Bill Chorley
Destination Fowington,Peter Longstaff-Tyrrell
Fighter Pilot, Bob Doe, DSO, DFC/Bar
Go Straight Ahead, 222 Sqadron, Ernie Burton
God, Honour and Country, Stanislaw Jozefiak
Lewes at War, 1939–45, Bob Elliston
Lions Rampant, Douglas McRoberts
McIndoe's Army, Peter Williams and Ted Harrison
Men of the Battle of Britain, Kenneth G. Wynn
Paddy, the life and times of, Patrick Barthropp, DFC AFC
Poles in Defence of Britain, Robert Gretzyngier
Spitfires over Sussex, David Rowland
The JG26 War Diaries, Donald Caldwell
The Mighty Eighth, Gerald Astor

Glossary

AA Anti-Aircraft
AC 1 Aircraftsman First Class
AFC Air Force Cross
ASR Air Sea Rescue
CGS Central Gunnery School
CO Commanding Officer
DFC Distinguished Flying Cross
DFM Distinguished Flying Medal
DSO Distinguished Service Order
E&RFTS Elementary and Reserve Flying Training School
FTS Flying Training School
OTU Operational Training Unit
PGW Pilot Gunnery Wing
RAFVR Royal Air Force Volunteer Reserve
RauxAF Royal Auxiliary Air Force

About the Author

David Rowland was brought up by his grandmother during the war in a terraced house in Brighton. He witnessed many of the bombs that dropped on the town. At the age of eight years, he and a friend were almost shot and killed when a Focke-Wulf 190 machine-gunned the street where they stood. It was reflecting on this incident that was to stimulate his interest in Brighton's war years, a subject in which some now consider him an expert.

His interest in wartime crashed aircraft first developed some seven years ago, and he considers himself very fortunate to be in contact with many wartime pilots and to be able to count them as friends. Indeed, he regards them all as 'huge stars,' firmly believing that he could never have done what they did – flown a fighter or bomber during the Second World War.

There are many more wartime stories that he would like to publish in due course. Some feature everyday folk who, although perhaps not so well known to the general public, nevertheless put their lives on the line in an effort to make the world a better place for us all.

Author's note

I would like to end this book about the wonderfully brave men whose stories I have told with the following words. I have borrowed them from Paddy Barthropp's book, called simply *Paddy*, and with his permission. They were written by his great friend Group Captain Brian Kingcombe, himself a great Battle of Britain pilot, responsible for destroying or damaging 30 enemy aircraft during 1940–41.

I believe these words could have been spoken by any pilot or aircrew member, and they certainly reflect the thoughts of those men lucky enough to have survived the fight against the enemy during the Second World War.

Wg.-Comdr. Brian Kingcombe.

'I lost many old friends as well as making many new ones, and the worst part was watching them die, spiralling down with a smudge of smoke, or breaking up, watching for the parachute to blossom: the relief when it did, the sick feeling when it didn't.'

Index